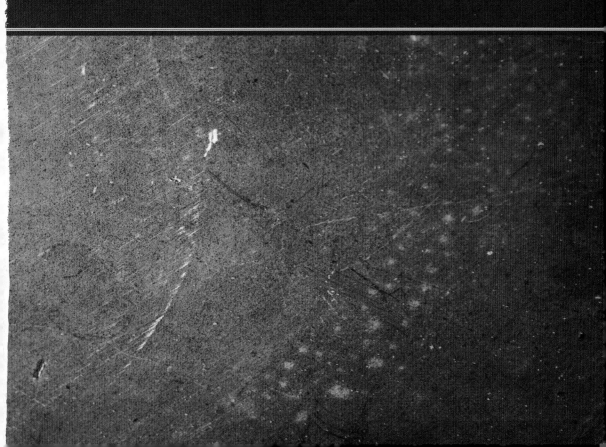

The

PALEO SLOW COOKER BIBLE

HEALTHY AND DELICIOUS FAMILY GLUTEN-FREE RECIPES

The

PALEO SLOW COOKER BIBLE

—AMELIA SIMONS—

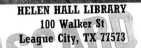

Skyhorse Publishing

Skyhorse Publishing books may be purchased in bulk at special discounts for sales promotion, corporate gifts, fund-raising, or educational purposes. Special editions can also be created to specifications. For details, contact the Special Sales Department, Skyhorse Publishing, 307 West 36th Street, 11th Floor, New York, NY 10018 or info@skyhorsepublishing.com.

Skyhorse® and Skyhorse Publishing® are registered trademarks of Skyhorse Publishing, Inc.®, a Delaware corporation.

www.skyhorsepublishing.com

10 9 8 7 6 5 4 3 2 1

Library of Congress Cataloging-in-Publication Data is available on file.

Cover design by
Cover photo credit

Print ISBN: 978-1-62873-743-1

Printed in China

Contents

Introduction

WELCOME TO PALEOLITHIC SLOW COOKER SOUPS AND STEWS

Some of my favorite dishes to cook in my slow cooker are hearty, delicious tasting, and wonderfully smelling soups and stews. There is just something comforting about a scrumptious bowl of soup that appeals to our senses as it nourishes our souls.

The aromas that fill our homes with special fragrances make soups and stews worth the time and effort to prepare them. Fortunately, using a slow cooker makes this effort rewarding. With just a short amount of time to put ingredients together in one pot, placing the lid on top, and setting the temperature, we are greeted at the end of the day with smells that alert us to a special treat awaiting.

So, come inside and wander through the recipes until you find one that piques your interest. Read through the list of ingredients, and imagine the enchanting smells that will fill the air as your slow cooker does its magic.

See an ingredient you don't have or don't like? No problem. Make a substitution. Improvise. That is what everybody else does. That is how favorites are created. You are limited only by your imagination, and it is the only thing standing between you and your next favorite meal!

By the way, **all recipes found in this cookbook use a 6-quart slow cooker**. This cookbook consists of recipes that will feed a family of five or six easily—depending upon the appetites of your crew. Raising three boys means I know what a big appetite is, so I have tried to make sure each recipe provides plenty for your family.

If you have any leftovers, you can always enjoy these recipes for lunches or another meal during the week. Like so many wonderful soups and stews, the flavors just seem to get better with age.

Enjoy, and may you and your slow cooker become best friends!

What Exactly Does Paleo Mean?

The Paleo way of eating includes various names like: Primal Diet, Cave Man Diet, Stone Age Diet, Hunter-Gatherer Diet, the Paleo Diet ™ and a few others.

In a nutshell, Paleolithic eating is attempting to eat as our ancestors once did. It is a diet consisting of high-protein, moderate-fat foods that are not processed, modified, or tampered with. It is living a lifestyle of eating foods that are low in carbohydrates such as lean meats, vegetables, fruits, good fats, and some starches.

Looking back thousands of years ago, our ancestors survived, and thrived, as hunter-gatherers. Our ancestors were muscular, agile, quite tall, athletic, and extremely versatile. Their diets consisted of meat and fish, nuts and seeds, fruits and vegetables.

While many years have passed, our genetic makeup has not changed much at all. We have certainly experienced many advances in technology that have made other forms of food available to us, such as grains, processed foods, and dairy. However, these food "advances" are actually not as easy for our bodies to digest as foods once were. Now many years later, man is often overweight, stressed, sleep deprived, lacking exercise, and dying of many diseases that experts say can often be prevented.

Apparently, a large part of our problem turns out to be due to agriculture! When farming became a huge part of our way of life for obtaining our food, we changed from hunter-gatherers to farmers. As a result, man began to settle down, formed different cultures and societies, and evolved into a world as we know it today.

Now, it seems as though our bodies have never properly adjusted to eating the grains produced from farming. Instead of loading up on meat, vegetables and seasonal fruits as our hunter-gatherer ancestors had to, we have become a species dependent upon grains. Foods like bread, pasta, rice, and corn have become a huge part of our diet.

I have read statistics that describe as many as 66% of us as being overweight while 33% of us are considered obese. In addition, if this is not bad enough, it appears as though these numbers are getting worse. Clearly, there is something terribly wrong with our eating habits and we need to do something differently.

The Paleolithic diet is all about making a lifestyle change whereby we go back to eating how we were biologically designed to eat. In doing so, we find ourselves returning to our genetic heritage, resulting in a healthier style of eating as soon as we do. Ultimately, the foods recommended in a Paleolithic diet provide our bodies with more efficient, long-lasting energy that also aid in burning fat, building muscle, improving sleep, and many other health benefits—all waiting to be discovered by individuals who adapt this way of eating and living.

What Are Some of the Things I Need to Know at the Start?

As you begin your journey into this healthier lifestyle, I want to give you some basic principles and approaches to keep in mind from the start. Knowing some of what you will encounter will make you an informed student and keep surprises to a minimum:

1. Paleo eating is not a diet. While it is certainly a change in your diet, consider it as a change in your lifestyle. Dedicate this next period of your life to focusing on becoming a healthier you. Read, make educated choices, and exercise—all with the mindset that these will be changes you can see yourself doing for the rest of your life.

2. Changes like what you will experience will happen one step at a time. Whether you go "cold turkey," or make the change to a Paleo lifestyle gradually, realize it does require **change**. Be patient with yourself, extend yourself grace on occasions when you mess up, but make a decision to change! After all, what has your present way of eating offered you up to at this point?

3. Spend time reading books and blogs about the Paleolithic lifestyle. Do not try to do this alone without a support system or virtual community. While a Paleolithic way of eating is gaining in popularity, it is still quite counter-cultural.

4. If you "fall off the wagon" at any time, do your best to avoid anything with gluten. It takes about two weeks of fasting from gluten for your body to recover from its influences on your system. We will talk more about how gluten affects your body in a later chapter.

5. A good place to begin making changes is at breakfast time. If you enjoy eggs, you already have a good handle on eating Paleo. Make them omega-3-enriched eggs and mix them in with some sautéed veggies like bell pep-

pers, mushrooms, and onions and you are on your way. If you would like other recipe ideas to get your mornings started off in the Paleolithic way, be sure to check out my recipe books entitled *4 Weeks of Fabulous Paleolithic Breakfasts*, and *4 MORE Weeks of Fabulous Paleolithic Breakfasts*. In these, you will find many recipes for frittatas, pancakes, and even grain-free muffins.

6. As you begin, be sure to read food labels carefully. Concentrate on whole foods like meats, fruits and vegetables as you begin. This will give you time to learn which foods and ingredients to avoid. Take time to learn terminology. Strive for the best foods you can afford like organic fruits and vegetables and grass-fed beef.

7. When it comes time to clean out your refrigerator, freezer, and pantry and restock them with paleo-friendly foods, be thorough and aggressive! If you do not have it in your home, you will not be tempted to eat it.

8. Do your best to plan so you have the ingredients you need. The time you spend planning your meals and shopping lists will ensure you have the ingredients necessary to succeed.

Now that you have some idea of the direction you are headed, let me share with you some basic information concerning meats, seafood, and eggs—important proteins involved in this new way of eating.

What About Meat, Seafood, and Eggs?

Meat, seafood, and eggs are perhaps the most important components of a Paleo way of eating. This is because these foods are the protein-building blocks necessary for good health and form much of the nutritional foundation a Paleo lifestyle is built upon.

Let's begin with meat: This category includes beef, pork, lamb, veal, elk, venison, and bison. When choosing any of these meats, the goal is to strive for grass-fed and pasture-raised organic meats whenever your budget allows. However, if grain-fed is the only option you have or the only one you can afford, do not fret about it. Strive for leaner cuts of meat and remove outer sections of fat before cooking. Because toxins in animals tend to be stored in their fat, removing this will diminish your intake.

Simply buy the best and leanest cuts of meat you can afford.

Whether or not bacon should be included in a Paleolithic diet is widely debated. Some consider it processed so they won't eat it. Others state that because the pig had a face, a mother and a father, it should be included in the list of meats. Ultimately, it is a decision you have to make. If you decide to enjoy this meat (as I do on occasion), try to purchase bacon that is nitrate and nitrite free.

Now concerning poultry: When choosing chicken, turkey, duck, goose, or pheasant, try to purchase pasture-raised poultry. This means these animals were allowed to roam about freely and consumed bugs and other insects in their diet rather than grains. If you cannot afford these, then try to purchase organic, free-range poultry as your next-best choice.

Next, let's talk about seafood: When it comes to trying to eat the healthiest seafood available, you will want to look for seafood that is labeled "wild-caught." This means the seafood contains healthy amounts of omega-3 fatty acids and was caught using sustainable and ethical fishing practices.

While there is a large array of seafood to choose from, lobster, shrimp, crab, scallops, Alaskan salmon, Mahi Mahi, tilapia, cod, mussels, clams, oysters, and Yellow fin tuna tend to be the most popular.

Finally, concerning eggs: Your best bet is to try to find a local source of pasture-raised chicken eggs. These come from chickens that have been allowed to roam outside of cages and feed freely on bugs. If these are not an option, look for omega-3 enriched eggs at your grocery store. These come from chickens that are fed a vegetarian diet while being supplemented with flax in their diet. Flax helps to increase the amount of omega-3 levels in the eggs.

As you have learned from this section, much of what you probably already eat is part of a Paleolithic diet so you may not have to relearn much going forward. If you are like me, you will probably spend your time in this area learning how to find grass-fed meat sources that are affordable. Fortunately, this type of meat is gaining popularity and is more readily available online and in some grocery stores, too. Like me, you will also have to decide if eliminating junk food from your diet makes it possible to afford better meat.

Now I'm going to talk with you about an area that will require some major changes from what you are used to with the Standard American Diet. It will require eliminating grains from your diet. Can't imagine how to do this? In the beginning, I couldn't imagine being able to either, but it is really quite possible and in the next section, I'd like to share with you why you should and how you can.

What Is the Problem with Grains?

Paleo eating is an aggressive attempt to remove processed foods from your diet. One of the biggest changes you will make when choosing this lifestyle is the removal of all grains. Initially, this may sound incredibly difficult or even impossible to do; however, with some help and further information, I believe you will find this possible and even beneficial to attain.

Grains are composed of carbohydrates, and carbohydrates are calorie-dense. Our bodies turn carbohydrates into glucose. This is a kind of sugar that is used for energy and various other tasks to help our bodies function. However, if these calories are not used immediately, they will inevitably turn into fat.

Some of the grains you will be trying to avoid include wheat, rye, barley, rice, oats, millet, and corn. Foods that contain high amounts of these grains include breads, pastas, baked goods, pancakes, biscuits, muffins, bagels, cereals, and many others.

Many grains contain gluten which is the large, water-soluble protein that creates the elasticity in dough. I have learned that researchers now believe that as many as one-third of humans are gluten-sensitive and even gluten-intolerant, and yet many are not even aware that they are. What this actually means is that their bodies react to gluten with an inflammatory response, often resulting in conditions like joint pain, acid reflux, dermatitis, digestive conditions, celiac disease, and several others.

Just out of curiosity, have you noticed all the "gluten-free" labeling on products that have started showing up in the marketplace? I don't think this is a coincidence! Apparently, many manufacturers and marketers are aware of what is happening to our health and are responding accordingly.

Another problem with grains is they contain lectins. Lectins are actually natural plant toxins that can inhibit healthy gastrointestinal function by interrupting nutrient absorption such as glucose, amino acids, fats, vitamins and minerals and others that normally make their way into our bloodstreams.

Additionally, lectin allows larger, undigested protein molecules to get into our bloodstream, which can become stuck on the outside of our healthy cells, rather than being broken down so healthy cells can absorb them. Consequently, when we get sick or the times when our bodies are trying to attack "enemy" cells, our bodies become confused by who the real "enemy" is.

Apparently, grains have evolved to the point where they actually try to keep themselves from being digested. As one author put it, "These lectins are not a fan of our gastrointestinal tract, thus preventing the tract from repairing itself from normal wear and tear." As you can see, eating grains can cause our digestive system all kinds of problems.

So, the bottom line where grains are concerned seems to be this: Grains are unhealthy and can actually be considered dangerous to your health on several levels. Not convinced? Just ask someone who has been diagnosed with Celiac disease.

Now, you may be wondering, "If grains are bad for me, what am I supposed to use for flour in cooking and baked goods?" As it turns out, nuts are not only enjoyed for snacking (more on this later), but they can be ground up and used as flour substitutes. Nuts such as almonds, pecans and coconuts are used widely in the Paleo community for making crusts, muffins, and breads. Admittedly, you will have to do some experimenting but many, including myself, have had great results changing over to these ingredients in cooking.

There is a great deal of information available through books and websites that explain the negative effects of grains in our diet. I encourage you to read further to give you a better understanding concerning this issue. Taking the time to learn more about grains and how they affect our bodies will help motivate you as you strive to eliminate them from your eating. As an added bonus, knowing how to effectively make substitutions for grains can actually help you lose weight as you begin to experience an overall sense of good health.

While eliminating grains has its challenges, you may find the next section to be a difficult task as well. In it, we will be discussing the topic of sugars—why they are mostly eliminated from our diets and which ones can be enjoyed on occasion.

Can I Still Eat Sugar?

Most of us seem to have some form of a sweet tooth. Whether it is sweetened coffee drinks, chocolate, cakes and cinnamon buns, we definitely like sugar. Why, even potatoes and white breads turn into sugar after they enter our digestive systems which may be another reason why we eat them as much as we do.

If you think you just can't live without sugar, I'm here to tell you that it is possible. I'm living proof. I happen to be one of those people who loves her chocolate, along with an occasional piece of cherry pie and sugary desserts. So, when I discovered that the basic rule for the Paleo lifestyle is to avoid all sugars, I wasn't too sure I could do this, but I have quite successfully and so can you.

In the category of sugar, you will find white sugar, high fructose corn syrup, candy, milk chocolate, soda, and artificial sweeteners. While sugar comes in many different forms such as sucrose, fructose, and lactose, each has its own path of destruction and causes damage to our bodies.

One of the important factors in deciding how foods affect your body and which ones are healthy for you can be determined by using a numbering system known as the Glycemic Index. The glycemic index—known as GI for short—is a way of ranking carbohydrates from 0 to 100. What this means is, the lower the number, the slower the absorption and rise in your insulin levels in your bloodstream will be. Foods with a high GI are rapidly digested and absorbed into your bloodstream as they cause higher fluctuations in your blood sugar and insulin levels.

On the other hand, low GI-foods result in slow digestion and absorption, resulting in gradual rises in your blood sugar and insulin levels. Additionally, this also offers benefits for weight control because low GI-foods help control your appetite and delay hunger.

Because fruits can vary greatly in their glycemic index numbers, it is important to become familiar with the ones that are rated high on this scale.

When they are, it means they contain a lot of natural sugars, causing your blood sugar and insulin levels to rise more than those rated with a lower number.

When you find yourself tempted to eat a sugary treat, I want you to know a few of the problems your body will encounter when you do. Knowledge is power and learning what I share with you about sugar in this section may be just what you need to fight off those sweet cravings we all get from time to time.

1. Sugar promotes weight gain because it causes fat storage.

2. Sugar decreases the secretion of a hormone called leptin. Leptin is essential for helping your body regulate your appetite.

3. A high intake of sugar over time can result in insulin resistance, often leading to Type II diabetes, as well as numerous other conditions involving your cardiovascular and nervous systems.

4. Sugar can simulate some of the same effect in your brain as some drugs do and can actually cause you to become addicted to it.

5. Did I happen to mention that sugar has calories, too?

When trying to eliminate sugar from your diet, it is important to learn the various names for it. Sugar has many aliases so it often hides in foods you may not even suspect like salad dressings, frozen vegetables, and many low-fat foods. Some of the labels used for sugar include the following names:

♦   Glucose
♦   Fructose
♦   Sucrose—otherwise known as table sugar
♦   Corn Syrup
♦   High Fructose Corn Syrup
♦   Honey. Honey consists of dextrose and fructose in a 1 to 1 ratio. If you decide to ever eat honey, which is permissible in a Paleolithic diet, be sure to consume raw honey instead of processed. Here's why: the glycemic index for raw honey is 30; for processed honey, it jumps to 75.

◆ Next, avoid processed maple syrup; however, pure maple syrup is allowed occasionally

◆ Finally, avoid molasses and agave nectar

As I wrap up this section, I would like to introduce you to coconut sugar as an alternative sweetener. While there really aren't any sweetening additives that are considered "primal," a new sweetener that has received positive reviews in the Paleo community, as of this writing, is coconut sugar. It is a one-to-one replacement for refined white sugar, but unlike table sugar, coconut sugar is rich in its nutritional content. It includes nutrients like magnesium, potassium, zinc, iron, B vitamins, and amino acids. In addition, the glycemic index for this natural sugar is low at only 35! However, please note, coconut sugar is *still sugar*! It is largely sucrose-based and does contain calories!

Now that we've covered two categories that can be tough to give up, let's move on to one that I believe you will find enjoyable and not difficult to do—fruits and vegetables.

Which Fruits and Vegetables Are Allowed?

Fruits and vegetables are a large part of the Paleo lifestyle, and thankfully, there is a wide variety to choose from which we will address in a moment. Ideally, you could grow your own produce. This would give you the freshest produce possible and allow you to know exactly what you are eating. However, for many, this is not an option. Instead, consider shopping at your local farmers' market and concentrate on buying the best organic products your budget can afford at your favorite grocery store.

An Another option available to many is participating in a CSA program. This stands for "community supported agriculture." These organizations enable individuals to help support local farmers in their area while receiving a share in the harvest. Be sure to check the Internet to see what options are available to you in your area.

Many authorities in the primal community stress the importance of only eating vegetables and fruits which are in season. Although not a hard-and-fast rule, I want to present a list of fruits and vegetables according to the seasons when they are most plentiful and nutritious.

Spring Harvest:

- Apricots
- Grapefruit
- Lemons
- Strawberries
- Artichokes
- Lettuce
- Mushrooms
- Spinach

- ◆ Asparagus
- ◆ Leeks
- ◆ Radishes
- ◆ Green onions
- ◆ Spring onions and
- ◆ Rhubarb

Summer Harvest:

- ◆ Apples
- ◆ Berries
- ◆ Cherries
- ◆ Melons
- ◆ Nectarines
- ◆ Peaches
- ◆ Mangoes
- ◆ Avocados
- ◆ Bell peppers
- ◆ Carrots
- ◆ Green beans
- ◆ Okra
- ◆ Tomatoes and
- ◆ Garlic

Fall Harvest:

- ◆ Broccoli
- ◆ Cauliflower

- Cranberries
- Grapes
- Limes
- Winter squash
- Kale
- Pumpkin
- Collard greens
- Arugula
- Brussels sprouts
- Swiss chard and
- Pomegranates

Winter Harvest:

- Celery
- Sweet potatoes
- Turnips
- Cabbage
- Beets
- Parsnips
- Onions
- Rutabagas
- Kiwis
- Mandarins
- Pears
- Citrus fruits and
- Clementines

If you are unable to grow your own food and CSA's are not an option, shopping at your local grocery store is still a great choice. Do your best to buy organic. Organically grown fruits and vegetables tend to have the least amount of chemicals and pesticides used during their production. Even if you cannot buy all organically-grown produce, consider buying organic for the following fruits and vegetables because these tend to absorb pesticides more readily than others:

- Grapes

- Cherries

- Peaches

- Apples

- Strawberries

- Nectarines

- Pears

- Celery

- Lettuce

- Bell peppers and

- Spinach

Vegetables are greatly encouraged in a Paleolithic diet and most can be eaten in unlimited quantities. Almost all vegetables offer excellent nutritional value and many contain high levels of antioxidants.

Vegetables provide a beautiful array of textures and colors in your diet which makes them eye appealing and appetizing. They can be extremely versatile when served with meats or enjoyed all by themselves.

Vegetables should be one of your main sources of carbohydrates because they are rich in vitamins, anti-inflammatory agents, minerals, and antioxidants. Additionally, they are low in calories so they can be eaten every day, as well as several times throughout each day.

The following list of vegetables are ones that contain the highest levels of antioxidants:

- Kale
- Onions
- Yellow squash
- Brussels sprouts
- Broccoli
- Red bell peppers
- Garlic
- Spinach
- Avocados
- Carrots
- Beets
- Cauliflower and
- Eggplant

Sugar found in fruit occurs naturally; hence the name, "Nature's candy." Many fruits offer nutritional benefits due to the levels of antioxidants and vitamins packed inside them. However, fruits come with a type of warning label if you are trying to lose weight. Because some fruits have a high sugar content, you will want to know which fruits pack the biggest "hit" on the glycemic index. Using this as a guideline, the following list contains those fruits that are lower on the GI scale and can be consumed daily:

- Blackberries
- Raspberries
- Strawberries
- Blueberries

- ♦ Goose berries
- ♦ Huckleberries
- ♦ Peaches
- ♦ Apples
- ♦ Pears
- ♦ Cherries
- ♦ Apricots and
- ♦ Figs

Fruits that are higher on the GI scale and should be eaten in moderation include:

- ♦ Pineapple
- ♦ Mangoes
- ♦ Melons such as watermelon and cantaloupe which are very high in their sugar content, and
- ♦ Papaya

In conclusion, eat dried fruits and drink fruit juices only on occasion. Because of the high concentration of sugar in dried fruits and fruit juices, these can spike your blood sugar levels and cause you to gain weight.

See, that section was pretty easy don't you think? Now let's move on to another area that is one of my favorites—nuts and seeds.

What About Nuts and Seeds?

Nuts and seeds offer protein and fat and can help satisfy hunger. This category of nutrition includes seeds and nuts like macadamias, Brazil nuts, hazelnuts, pistachios, walnuts, almonds, pecans, cashews, squash seeds, sunflower seeds, pumpkin seeds, flax seeds, and pine nuts.

If you were to approach this area of eating like our hunter-gatherer ancestors would have, it would have taken a lot of work and time just to end up with a handful of shelled nuts to eat. In addition, they would have been consumed in limited quantities and not very often.

Be aware that nuts are high in their fat content which makes them high in calories, so be sure to limit your intake if you desire to lose weight.

Nuts that are ground into butters make a great snack and are easy to make. By putting most any nut into a blender or food processor, along with a little coconut oil and sea salt, why you can make a fabulous tasting spread for celery, apples, and many others. Be sure to refrigerate these once you make them and store their containers upside down to keep the oil from floating to the top.

Flours made from grinding up nuts are a great substitute for regular flours used in making pizza crusts, cookies, crackers, piecrusts, and other flour-based products. Some of the products you will find used as alternatives for baking in many Paleolithic recipes are ones like pecan meal, blanched almond flour, almond meal, coconut flour, and flax seed meal.

A Note about Peanuts:

Because peanuts are actually legumes and not really nuts at all, they should be avoided. They actually have the highest concentration of aflatoxins which are dangerous metabolites produced by certain mold varieties, and are heavily sprayed with pesticides during their growing season.

If you happen to be allergic to some of the nuts mentioned in this chapter, you will need to do more research and talk extensively with your health care provider.

Now let's delve into the next category of foods that you may have been wondering about which happens to be all about dairy products.

Are Dairy Products Okay?

This area is one that many Paleolithic eaters are divided upon. Many folks stay away from dairy products completely because they are lactose intolerant, meaning their bodies cannot handle the digestion of the sugar found in dairy products known as lactose without negative consequences. These uncomfortable side effects consist of symptoms like bloating, cramping, and diarrhea. While there are those who are intolerant and suffer with autoimmunity issues, there are also those who simply dislike dairy.

If we continue to look to the hunter-gatherer as our role model, we would notice that they did not drink milk once they were weaned as a child. Milk was only consumed when they were babies from their mothers. Because of this model, many have come to believe that our bodies were not designed for the massive amounts of dairy consumption that is practiced today.

As you ponder this thought, here are a few guidelines to help you further understand this category of food:

1. While many Paleo eaters do not eat dairy products, many others do. It is one of those "gray areas" existing within this community. If you can tolerate dairy and want to enjoy it on occasion, many would offer their blessing. They would advise you to start with cultured butter, yogurts that are plain and not fruit flavored, kefir, clotted milks, and aged cheeses. These items are fermented products, causing a drastic reduction in lactose and casein levels of the dairy products.

2. Next would come raw, high-fat dairy products like raw butter and cream because they are minimally processed and are good sources of saturated fat. Most of these are free from lactose and casein and are best if they come from grass-fed, pasture-fed animals.

3. Avoid homogenized and pasteurized milks. If you buy them, make them organic, hormone and antibiotic-free milk. As an alternative to milk, many

substitute unsweetened almond milk and coconut milk in place of cow's milk.

4. Grass-fed butter is considered okay, although many suggest using ghee that is clarified butter with the milk solids removed. By doing so, you are now consuming it as a fat instead of dairy.

5. If you want to eat cheeses on occasion, be sure they are aged cheeses. The aging process decreases the levels of lactose and casein in the cheese, making them better tolerated by those who are sensitive to lactose and casein.

6. Because nuts are allowed, unsweetened almond milk and coconut milk are often used as substitutes for dairy.

Personally, I am not a milk drinker, but I am one of those Paleo eaters that choose to enjoy some dairy on occasion. At one time I fasted from any dairy products for a total of 60 days. When I reintroduced dairy into my diet, I did not have any noticeable reactions at all. So for me, I am fine with some cream in my coffee and butter on my paleo-style muffins. I encourage you to do the same. Many do not know how dairy affects them until they have eliminated it from their diet for a period of time, and then reintroduce it to evaluate its effects upon their body.

Since "going Paleo," I now use aged cheeses like cheddars and Parmesan (Parmigiano Reggiano is good!) I continue to use cream in my coffee like I always have. Besides, a mushroom-crusted pizza just isn't the same without some cheese melted on top! I am not saying whether or not this is right or wrong for you, but it works for me.

Right now you may be wondering what you can substitute for regular cow's milk. Let me offer a few suggestions.

1. Coconut milk: If you want to find a substitute for cream and other milk products as I have done, then using coconut milk is a great alternative. Canned coconut milk is a perfect substitute and is not difficult to find. You can use this in your recipes in place of heavy cream, half and half, and cow's milk. Use it in soups, stews, and even in your coffee.

Coconut milk actually is a great source for lauric acid that is essential for your immune system and one of the most beneficial essential fatty acids your body needs.

2. Almond milk: Although almond milk is often a preference to cow's milk, it is high in omega-6 fatty acids because it is made from nuts. Most people already have elevated omega-6 levels in their bodies, so it is not something you want to drink regularly. Instead, enjoy it by the tablespoon-full in your coffee or tea, but do not resort to making it a substitute for your regular milk-drinking habits.

3. Heavy cream: While heavy cream is a dairy product, heavy cream is actually mostly fat. If you buy organic, grass-fed heavy cream, you will benefit from the good omega-3 fats found in the cream.

Like other dairy products, let your body tell you if cream is causing you any problems or not. If you find yourself feeling bloated or sluggish after using it in recipes or in your cup of java, consider substituting it with coconut milk instead.

Eliminating dairy products or learning to use substitutions will take some time, but in the long run, your body will benefit from it.

In the next section, I am going to help you understand which kinds of oils are good for you to use in your cooking and for your dietary needs.

Which Fats Can I Eat?

Fats are essential ingredients in our diet. Not only are they necessary for certain bodily functions, but they make food taste good. The key is to make them *healthy fats*.

In this section I am going to present you with a short list of the healthy fats and oils you should use in your daily eating and cooking—even if you decide not to join the Paleo community.

The list of healthy fats consists of the following:

◆ Ghee, also known as clarified butter

◆ Grass-fed butter

◆ Olive oil

◆ Sesame oil

◆ Coconut butter

◆ Coconut oil

◆ Lard

◆ Tallow

◆ Avocado oil and

◆ Macadamia nut oil

Personally, since I have given up grains, I don't use much butter. I do use it in a few recipes and I like it melted on some of my vegetables, but I definitely have cut back tremendously on my butter consumption.

Organic, grass-fed butter has some healthy properties and can be a good source of fat, too. If you currently use butter for cooking, try using coconut oil for high heat cooking and olive oil for lower heat settings instead.

From my reading, I would say that if you do not suffer from any sort of autoimmune issue and are otherwise healthy, adding butter occasionally to your food should be fine. I would also offer the suggestion of eating clarified butter. This is butter that has been put through a clarification process and is actually easy to make at home. Just heat up your butter over a low heat until the milk solids have settled to the bottom and the froth floats on top. Gently remove the froth, scoop out the clear liquid, but do not disturb the sediment on the bottom. This will eliminate most of the milk solids from the butter that usually give people troubles with digestion.

Avoid any products that include shortening, margarines, canola oil, soybean oil, cottonseed oil, peanut oil, corn oil, sunflower oil, and any product with "partially hydrogenated" in the ingredients. Plus, be sure to check the label on your mayonnaise so you know which type of oil was used in its processing.

What Herbs and Spices are Recommended?

There are many wonderful herbs and spices available on the market today. These add life and flavors to your dishes. While fresh is often best, it may be difficult for you to find them or you may desire to use dried instead. You will find wonderful spices and herbs that have been dried and packaged for your enjoyment. Simply learn how to measure dry verses fresh in your recipes.

The thing you will want to pay attention to in this area is the ingredients label. While pure herbs and spices do not have additives, herb and spice mixes often contain gluten and other ingredients. Find ones you can trust and enjoy.

Some of the flavorful spices, herbs, and seasonings you will want to try are ones like:

◆ Basil

◆ Celery seed

◆ Cinnamon

◆ Cumin

◆ Fennel seed

◆ Garlic

◆ Lemon

◆ Lime

◆ Onion powder

◆ Oregano

◆ Paprika

◆ Parsley

◆ Pepper

◆ Rosemary

- ◆ Salt

- ◆ Shallots and

- ◆ Thyme

With so many wonderful choices, there is never any reason for your food to taste bland and boring. Get creative. Use herbs and spices in all your cooking. They will add life and flavor to your dishes.

WHAT OTHER FOODS AM I ALLOWED TO ENJOY?

As we are coming down the home stretch on the different categories of foods to enjoy or avoid, we only have a few left. Once we cover these, it will be time to move on to organizing and shopping.

Sweet potatoes and yams are classified as tubers. They are higher in calories and carbs, so they should only be eaten occasionally. White and red potatoes are to be avoided.

When it comes to snacks, you can enjoy foods like olives, nuts and nut butters, dried fruits, beef and turkey jerky, fresh berries, and cooked leftover meats. Be advised that seldom are you going to find processed snack foods that are paleo-friendly.

Finally, in the category of beverages, all spokespersons agree that water is best and should be your main choice of beverage. Coconut water has also become a great drink, especially for enjoying after a heavy workout. Generally, tea is fine, and there continues to be some continuing discussions concerning the health benefits of alcohol and coffee.

If you are going to drink alcohol, enjoy those that do not require sugary mixtures. Also, try not to drink right before going to bed because it can disturb your sleep.

Finally, as you may have guessed, beverages that require sweeteners like sugars or artificial sweeteners are highly discouraged.

Tips on Grocery Shopping and Filling Your Pantry

As you are beginning to learn and understand the changes involved in switching to the Paleo lifestyle, you are now ready to take some action. There are certain steps you will need to take, foods you will need to eliminate from your pantry and refrigerator, and foods you will want to add to your shopping list.

♦   Begin this exercise by grabbing a large garbage bag and heading for your pantry or storage cabinets.

♦   Get rid of every single processed food you find there. This includes items like rice, pasta, potato chips, beans, bread, cereals, pretzels, candy, sodas, cake mixes, white flour, sugar, and artificial sweeteners.

♦   If any product is unopened and still usable, consider donating it to your local food bank or your church's pantry. And some of what you will find will be food items you should have gotten rid of a long time ago.

♦   Once you have finished, your cabinets or pantry shelves will look bare. From now on, you will notice that not many Paleolithic foods can be stored in your pantry. Most foods will need to be refrigerated or frozen.

♦   Next, it is time to go to your refrigerator. Get rid of all the salad dressings and condiments that contain sugars. Pick up every single item in there and read the label. When you are done, you should only have items like fresh veggies, eggs, unprocessed meats, fruits, mustard and salsa.

♦   If you decide that dairy is something you should eliminate as well, be sure to discard the milk, cheeses, butter, and the half and half for your coffee.

♦   The same drill goes for the freezer. Any prepackaged foods like vegetables with sauces, TV dinners, frozen bread rolls, pizzas, ice cream and others get tossed if they contain grains, sweeteners, and other additives that are not allowed.

Ridding your home of food items like those mentioned above can be tough, but by doing so, you have now eliminated any temptation to backslide while you are at home, meaning your willpower will not have to work as hard as if they remained.

Eliminating sauces such as soy sauce that contains gluten and added sugars may require further research on your part. Give yourself time to get the information you need to make wise choices. As you progress, be sure to do some studying about the tricky names for gluten and sugars so you can rid your home of forbidden hidden ingredients.

After you have dejunked your refrigerator and pantry, you need a plan of action. You need to know what items you should buy the next time you go grocery shopping. Obviously, much of this depends upon what your menus look like. Remember to start simply. Prepare meals that are mostly a protein with fresh vegetables and fruits. This will give you time to keep studying.

As your confidence builds, substitute items you normally eat with new Paleo food items. For example, try using spaghetti squash in place of pasta. Top your grilled burger with fresh salsa instead of ketchup. Have an egg frittata for dinner that includes fresh mushrooms, bell peppers, and onions.

As you make your list for the grocery store, there are certain items you will want to keep on hand in your pantry and refrigerator. The following list is one you will become familiar with as you continue with this way of eating.

For your pantry, purchase:

◆ A wide variety of spices

◆ Almond butter

◆ Almond meal

◆ Almond flour

◆ Raw almonds

- Raw pecans
- Raw walnuts
- Coconut flour
- Coconut flakes
- Canned coconut milk
- Diced tomatoes
- Tomato paste
- Gluten-free chicken broth
- Canned Alaskan salmon that states it is wild-caught
- Canned tuna
- Beef jerky without added sugars and preferably made from grass-fed beef
- Canned chicken
- Apple cider vinegar
- Dijon mustard
- Dry mustard
- Chicken stock
- Beef stock
- Coconut oil
- Olive oil
- Olives
- Artichoke hearts
- Jalapenos
- Canned green chilies
- Sun-dried tomatoes

- ◆ Unsweetened dried apricots, bing cherries, and figs
- ◆ Pure maple syrup
- ◆ Raw honey and
- ◆ Coconut sugar

For your refrigerator, purchase items such as:

- ◆ Fresh fruits and vegetables
- ◆ Omega-3 enriched eggs—preferably from free range chickens
- ◆ Grass-fed ground beef
- ◆ Free range chicken
- ◆ Nitrite and nitrate-free bacon
- ◆ Apples
- ◆ All kinds of berries
- ◆ Lemons
- ◆ Limes
- ◆ Spinach
- ◆ Cucumbers
- ◆ Carrots
- ◆ Kale
- ◆ Lettuces—Be sure to avoid iceberg lettuce and
- ◆ Salsa

As you shop more and read further, you will discover items that are not included on this list, like nuts and seeds that you can add to your shopping list. Additionally, you may have noticed that most of these items are usually found along the periphery of most grocery stores. Just think of the time this way of shopping will save you because you won't have to go down so many of the aisles anymore!

In the beginning, allow this list to guide you as you begin your new way of shopping and eating. While you may have thought eating like a hunter-gatherer would be difficult, it actually simplifies your grocery shopping.

Additional Tips and Advice

Like everyone else who who has gone before you, you will find some things easily accomplished while others will take some work. Remember, you are making a lifestyle change and that requires some unique challenges.

In this section, I simply want to offer you some additional advice, words of encouragement, and things I have discovered for myself and have incorporated into my life. I hope you find them helpful as well.

1. As you begin, be nice to yourself! Do not focus on your failures, but rather on your victories. Switching to a new way of eating is huge. Do the best you can and do not beat yourself up when you blow it.

2. Read. Educate yourself about primal eating. More and more information is becoming available as more people adopt this healthy lifestyle.

3. Plan your meals and shopping. By doing this, you will not find yourself without a critical ingredient you need for making a specific recipe.

4. Especially in the beginning, keep your meals simple.

5. Start thinking, "Dinner for breakfast." Because you are eliminating grains from your diet, you have to change your way of thinking about breakfast. While eggs are a logical choice, so is meatloaf and steak, along with salads and soups. Don't get hung up on what time of day it is.

6. Chop your vegetables ahead of time. Take some time during the week to clean, peel and chop your produce. This will make preparations faster and easier when the time for making your meals comes around.

7. Prepare extra servings when you cook. Leftover proteins and servings of entrees make great lunches and possibilities for breakfasts.

8. Try setting aside an hour on the weekends to plan your meals. Look at your

family's schedule. Make simple meals when you know it is going to be a busy day.

9.   Consider doing your grocery shopping on the weekends when you have a "break in the action" from your weekday commitments.

10. While you are getting used to Paleo eating, follow new recipes carefully. Once you feel comfortable with the changes, start creating your own recipes. That is what I did and it is fun!

For some, starting a Paleo lifestyle is easy while others may have a difficult time imagining giving up breads, pastries, and sweets. If there are foods you are not ready to give up, substitutions you are not ready to make, or find it difficult to afford organic produce and grass-fed beef, do not worry.

Making even a few changes will cause you to see some positive results. Often it starts by sleeping better, losing a little bit of weight, or experiencing relief from joint pain. These small changes often motivate people to make more changes leading toward a healthier lifestyle.

Here are a few other thoughts and suggestions to help you in making healthier changes:

1. Try the 80/20 rule: Several well-known spokespersons in the Paleolithic movement preach the 80/20 rule. This means be strict and eat really well 80% of the time, and then give yourself permission to splurge or treat yourself on occasion the other 20% of the time. One guru likes to eat really well during the week by being strict in his eating, then gives himself a day on the weekend to eat whatever he wants—things like cheeseburgers, bagels, and ice cream. Allowing yourself a chance to "get it out of your system" often helps you stay on track the rest of the week. Personally, I'm not disciplined enough to go back and forth, but this does encourage me for the times when I slip and indulge.

2. Transition gradually: If the thought of eating one way and changing to another way the next day sounds impossible or is not your style, try transitioning gradually. Over the course of a month or so, gradually finish off the foods you know you are not going to buy in the future and begin to replace them with wholesome foods.

Challenge yourself to only shop the perimeter of the store. This will keep you from replacing items in your pantry like pastas, pretzels, and cereals.

The biggest problem I see with this approach is it delays the benefits you could enjoy if you made the transition to Paleo eating quicker.

3. Cold turkey: While this approach may stretch you and often requires making many changes at once, it will also allow you to experience healthier changes quicker. Going cold turkey requires a big commitment on your part, but as I see it, your health is worth it.

What Might I Expect as I Begin the Paleolithic Diet?

Depending upon how you were eating before you decided to eat like our ancestors, there are some symptoms you may experience. Certainly, these do not hold true for everybody beginning this new journey, but being aware of them will help you know what lies ahead so you are not alarmed by any of them.

1. In the first two to three weeks, you may have some withdrawal symptoms like headaches and sluggishness. Much of this will be due to eliminating carbs and sugars from your diet. Because these symptoms have become commonplace, this experience has been labeled, "carb flu."

2. You may experience a loss of energy.

3. You may feel tired.

4. You may experience weakness.

5. You may not feel very productive.

Because your body may have been relying on sugars and starches for energy, you need to give yourself time to retrain your body. Do your best to fight the urge to eat sweets and starches. Also, try to avoid eating out if you can so you are not tempted to eat breads and potatoes that often accompany meats and vegetables.

Once your body has a chance to detox for several days, you should begin to notice some great things happening.

6. Your energy level should begin to return. In addition, it should remain more constant throughout the day.

7. You should not feel as hungry as often as you used to when you ate carbs and sugars for energy.

8. Cravings for unhealthy foods should begin to diminish as you fuel your body with healthy meats and vegetables.

9. Your sleeping should improve because now you are fueling your body with healthy proteins and fats.

10. You might actually see the numbers on the scale go down. Now that you are eating healthy foods that stick with you longer and you aren't stuffed with empty calories, your body will run and work more efficiently. If not, many find their clothes begin to fit better.

While these are just a few of the most common changes that happen for people switching to a Paleo lifestyle and diet, you can find other things that have happened to people through their testimonies all over the Internet.

Note from the Author—What Paleo Means to Me

I have become a big fan of the Paleo way of eating because I have seen such great results in my own life. When I started this journey, I could not imagine a day without my homemade cinnamon swirl bread made with freshly ground flour and lathered with real butter. However, now I cannot imagine going back to that.

Paleo eating makes a great deal of sense to me. As human beings, we were designed with teeth for chewing meats, nuts, and so many other foods. Nowadays, when you hear about all the bad research that is coming out about grains, it makes it even easier for me to stay away from them. While there are a few areas where other Paleo eaters are more dedicated than I, I have taken the plunge and have absolutely no plans to go back to how I used to eat.

Aside from giving up grains, which was probably the biggest challenge for me in the beginning, I have thoroughly enjoyed the simplicity of eating this way. Once I became familiar with the basic guidelines and made some substitutions for pastas and pizza, it has become a lifestyle that has not been complicated—especially when it comes to grocery shopping.

I hardly ever have to go down the aisles of the grocery store anymore except for household items like paper goods and coffee. That's right. I did not give up my love for coffee and I still put half and half in it to make it look pretty, but I have given up the artificial sweeteners I used to use in it! You, too, can learn to just shop the perimeter of the store and not need to go down the middle aisles very often. Paleo eating really has made grocery shopping easier and faster.

Another aspect I have noticed is I can eat whatever I want—whenever I want it. If I do not feel like having breakfast until lunchtime—that's okay. If I want to eat a hamburger for breakfast, I do. If I eat a big breakfast consisting of a southwestern omelet with bacon and do not feel like eating again until dinner—then I don't. Eating like this has definitely allowed me freedom from watching the clock or keeping track of how many servings I have of this and that. I really have enjoyed this way of "stress-free" eating.

Finally, I encourage you to give this change in lifestyle a sincere effort. Knowing what it has done for me personally causes me to get excited about sharing this information with family and friends. Like so many other things in life—when you have something good happen to you, you want to share it with others. Paleo eating works and ultimately, it is not hard!

Just try it for yourself and experience the results first hand. And when you do, I believe the results will convince you and you will become an enthusiastic Paleo follower as well.

A Few Ground Rules as We Get Started

Living a Paleolithic lifestyle and adapting this way of eating comes with a few ground rules. The basic overview for eating Paleolithic is this:

- Lots of meats
- Lots of vegetables
- Nuts and seeds
- Some fruit
- Some dairy (unless you have lactose problems or have chosen not to eat dairy)
- Little or no sugar
- No grains

For some, this may seem extremely restrictive, but for many who have adapted this way of eating, these guidelines have caused them to experience some improved signs of health— for some it has been significant.

As you go through my cookbook, I want to make you aware of some overall guidelines and try to make my intentions clear from the beginning.

1. Whenever your budget allows, try to buy proteins that are grass-fed, organic, pastured, free-range, and wild-caught. I will not be specifying these particular kinds of ingredients in the recipes because I know these types of proteins can be difficult for many people to purchase. With that said, always try and buy the leanest cuts of meat you can afford. Remove excess fat before cooking, and drain the fat from fattier meats after you cook them and before adding them to your slow cooker.

2. Try to use locally grown produce whenever possible. You would be amazed at how much cheaper it can be as well as healthier.

3. For sautéing and for preparing your slow cooker, coconut oil is an excellent choice for fat. It can withstand high temperatures and tastes great in recipes. Also, feel free to use grass-fed, organic butter or ghee. While olive oil is an excellent choice of oil, it oxidizes when heated, so it is best to reserve its use for drizzling and garnishing dishes that are already cooked or for salads and cold foods.

4. If you see a recipe you would like to try, but it contains some ingredients you don't think you like, omit them or substitute something else for them. There really is no "one right way" with slow cooker recipes. This is your chance to get creative!

5. You will see very little sweeteners included in the recipes here. (There are some used in the quick bread recipes). I try to stay away from sugar as much

as possible. Occasionally, if I use any sugar at all, it tends to be a small amount of raw honey where some liquid is needed, or I use coconut sugar when a dry ingredient is necessary. However, for almost all these recipes, including the section on quick breads (or muffins), sweetening is optional because there is no yeast involved. The end product is strictly a preference of taste.

6. Personally, I do eat a few dairy products. I use half and half in my coffee, and I enjoy some cheeses on occasion. I'm not a milk drinker at all, so any dairy products I consume are usually in the form of aged cheeses and cream in my coffee. The only "milk" used in these recipes is coconut milk, and you can use almond milk if you wish, and one recipe calls for shredded aged cheese IF you desire.

Tips on Adapting Favorite Soups and Stews to Slow Cooker Methods

Over the years, I have enjoyed taking some of my favorite family soup and stew recipes from years gone by and adapting them to use in my slow cooker. While this is not difficult to do, it does require some experimentation. If you find that you desire to do the same with some of your favorites, here are some things you will need to consider:

♦ The amount and size of the ingredients used
♦ Cooking temperatures used
♦ Amount of liquid needed
♦ Cooking times necessary

Unlike some traditional soup and stew recipes, slow cooker dishes are often delicious—no matter what you did to them. So, although most of your dishes will turn out successfully, let me give you a few tips and suggestions on what to do when converting your favorite soups and stews to slow cooker methods.

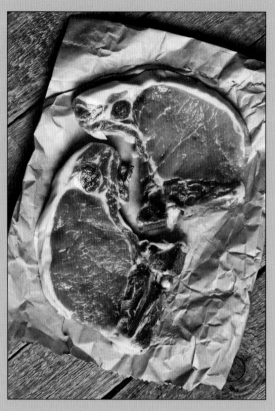

1. **Precook ground beef, stew meat, and any diced meat pieces before placing in your slow cooker.** The taste and final appearance of the dish is often enhanced when you do this beforehand. Although this isn't a rule that has to be followed every time (sometimes there just isn't time or you just don't feel like it), it can result in a richer flavor of the finished product.

2. **Consider cutting the liquid called for in half, except for soup recipes.** With recipes traditionally cooked on the stovetop or even in the oven, liquid can evaporate out. However, with a slow cooker, much of the liquid is trapped inside. Additionally, many foods like mushrooms and foods with high water contents will actually add to the amount of liquid in your slow cooker, so adjust the liquid amounts to your liking. This will take some experimentation to get it the consistency you desire.

3. **Consider sautéing foods like onions, mushrooms, and peppers on the stovetop before putting into the slow cooker.** If you are making a soup, this step can be skipped; however, for stews where you want them to be on the thicker side, consider sautéing first.

4. **Place the densest ingredients on the bottom.** When cooking dense foods like carrots, sweet potatoes, and squashes, place these closest to the bottom and along the sides where they will receive the most heat.

5. **Try to cut ingredients the same size.** Whether you are slicing or dicing, cutting ingredients that are equal in size will help with uniform cooking.

6. **Add herbs and spices near the end.** If using ground herbs and spices, consider adding these near the end of cooking since they tend to dissipate and can lose their flavors when you add them at the beginning. If using whole herbs, you can add these at the beginning because they release their flavors over time and work well with slow cooking.

7. **If you are able to tolerate dairy and want to use milk or cheese products in your recipes, add these near the end of cooking.** While many Paleolithic eaters don't consume dairy products, others do. If you are one of those who do, realize dairy products are affected in slow cooking. Because milk products tend to separate or curdle after cooking for long periods of time, it is best to add them in the last hour of cooking.

8. **Add seafood and nuts close to the end of cooking.** Seafood and fish tend to cook quickly, so these should be added in the later stages of cooking. If adding any nuts to your soup or stew, add these at the end or wait until the dish is served and add as a garnish.

Basic Beef and Chicken Broth Recipes

One of the ingredients called for in many soup and stew recipes is beef or chicken broth. While you can certainly buy prepared ones in cartons or dry ones you reconstitute, I find it is easy to make my own using my slow cooker. Not only is it cheaper, but I also know what is in them.

Once you have cooked the broth and strained out the bones and vegetables, it is easy to freeze the broths in small containers or even ice cube trays. For most ice cube trays, one cube is equivalent to two tablespoons or one-eighth of a cup. This is handy to know when you are preparing a recipe.

Below are the two basic recipes—one for beef and one for chicken. For beef broth, soup bones make a great tasting broth but can be a little tricky to find. Ask your butcher if he can obtain some for you. If you fix a roast that has a bone in it, save it and store it in your freezer until you are ready to use it. I have even seen places where you can buy them online.

Keep in mind when making these broths that there really aren't any exact measurements of ingredients. You simply put in whatever bones, carrots, celery, and so forth you have on hand or want to use up, cover with water, and let her cook for a long time.

Feel free to add or take out any ingredients you wish when making these delicious broths. The tastes are strictly up to you.

Note: These two recipes can also be used to make a vegetable stock, turkey stock, venison stock, and even a fish stock. The sky is the limit!

BEEF BROTH

Ingredients:

- 6 pounds of raw beef bones (bones with some meat attached)
- 3 carrots, cut into thick slices
- 2 celery stalks, cut into thick slices
- 2 onions, peeled then halved
- 2 teaspoons dried thyme leaves
- 4 garlic cloves, minced
- Any other seasonings, like salt and pepper

Directions:

1. Turn your 6-quart slow cooker on LOW as you begin to gather your ingredients.
2. Place any beef bones, minced garlic, carrots, onions, celery, and any other root vegetables into your slow cooker.
3. Add any seasonings, like salt, pepper, and so forth, to your liking.
4. Cover all the ingredients with water and cook for 24 hours.
5. Allow the broth to cool.
6. Strain the ingredients.
7. If you refrigerate the broth and allow the fat to harden on top, you can remove this easily and discard it.
8. Use in your favorite slow cooker recipe or store in containers or ice cube trays and freeze.

CHICKEN BROTH

Ingredients:

- 6 pounds of raw chicken parts (bones, giblets, skin, and some meat)
- 3 carrots, cut into thick slices
- 2 celery stalks, cut into thick slices
- 2 onions, peeled then halved
- 2 teaspoons dried thyme leaves
- 4 garlic cloves, minced
- Any other seasonings, like salt and pepper

Directions:

1. Turn your 6-quart slow cooker on LOW as you begin to gather your ingredients.
2. Place any chicken bones, carrots, celery, onions, thyme, garlic, and any other root vegetables and seasonings into a slow cooker.
3. Cover all the ingredients with water and cook for 24 hours.
4. Allow the broth to cool.
5. Strain the ingredients.
6. If you refrigerate the broth and allow the fat to harden on top, you can remove this easily and discard it.
7. Use in your favorite slow cooker recipe or store in containers or ice cube trays and freeze.

Beef Soups and Stews

BEEF STEW AND CABBAGE

If a nice hearty stew is what you are looking to fix for dinner one night, this one will do nicely. It has substance, has great flavor, and will satisfy even the hungriest eaters in your home.

Ingredients:

- 2 pounds ground beef
- 2 large onions, diced
- 5 carrots, peeled and sliced
- 1 head of cabbage, chopped (red adds color)
- 1 large eggplant, peeled and cubed (optional)
- 1 large can diced tomatoes
- 6 cups of chicken or beef broth
- 3 cups of water
- 1 teaspoon turmeric
- 4 garlic cloves, minced
- ½ teaspoon ground ginger
- 1 teaspoon cinnamon
- ¼ cup fresh basil, chopped
- ¼ cup fresh chives, chopped
- 2 teaspoons cumin
- 1 tablespoon sea salt
- 2 teaspoons coarse black pepper

Directions:

1. Turn your slow cooker on to HIGH while you prepare your ingredients.
2. In a large skillet on your stovetop, brown the ground beef along with the onions.
3. Place the browned beef and onions into your slow cooker.
4. Add the carrots, cabbage, eggplant, and tomatoes.
5. Gently pour in the broth and water.
6. Add the turmeric, garlic, ginger, and cinnamon and stir gently.
7. Cover and continue to cook on HIGH for 4 hours, or turn your slow cooker down to LOW and cook for 7 to 8 hours.
8. About 30 minutes before you plan to serve the stew, add the basil, chives, cumin, salt, and pepper, and stir to blend.
9. Replace the lid and heat through for 30 to 45 minutes.
10. Serve.

BEEF AND MUSHROOM STEW

I really enjoy mushrooms, so I use them in many of my recipes. If you like them, try this recipe with some different kinds of mushrooms. Maybe you will find you like them better than you thought. If not, feel free to eliminate them from this stew, but let me tell you, you will be missing out on some great flavors.

Ingredients:

- 4 garlic cloves, minced
- 2 onions, peeled and sliced
- 8 ounces whole shiitake mushrooms
- 8 ounces baby Portobello mushrooms
- 16 ounces sliced button mushrooms
- 3 pounds beef stew meat (brown on stovetop if you wish)
- 3 sweet potatoes, peeled and cubed
- 4 cups chicken or beef broth
- ⅔ cup balsamic vinegar
- 3 bay leaves
- 3 tablespoons onion powder
- 1 tablespoon dried rosemary
- 2 teaspoons dried sage
- 2 teaspoons dried parsley
- 1 tablespoon salt
- 2 teaspoons pepper

Directions:

1. Turn your slow cooker on HIGH while you prepare your ingredients.
2. Place the garlic, onions, and mushrooms on the bottom of the slow cooker.
3. Put the stew beef on top of the mushrooms, followed by the sweet potato cubes.
4. Pour the broth over the meat and potatoes.
5. Add the vinegar and bay leaves.
6. At this point you can put the remaining spices on top of the ingredients or wait until 45 minutes to 1 hour before serving to put them in.
7. Turn the slow cooker down to LOW and cook for 7 to 8 hours.

HEARTY CHILI

Say the word "chili" at my house, and the troops come running. They know it is going to be good because they've been smelling it for hours. Next time you have a crew to feed and you want something yummy, this dish will do the trick.

Ingredients:

♦   2 tablespoons coconut oil

♦   8 stalks of celery, sliced

♦   6 garlic cloves, minced

♦   2 large onions, diced

♦   4 pounds ground beef

♦   4 teaspoons cumin

♦   2 tablespoons chili powder

♦   4 teaspoons thyme

♦   24 ounces of your favorite salsa

♦   2 (14.5 ounce) cans of diced tomatoes

♦   3 (7 ounce) cans of green chilies

♦   2 tablespoons sea salt

Directions:

1. Turn on your slow cooker to HIGH so it can heat up while you are preparing your ingredients.
2. On the stovetop, use a large skillet to melt the coconut oil.
3. Put the celery, garlic, and onions into the skillet and sauté until tender.
4. Transfer to your slow cooker.
5. Now add the ground beef to the skillet and brown the beef.
6. Place the browned beef into the slow cooker.
7. Pour in the remaining ingredients and stir gently.
8. Turn the slow cooker down to LOW and cook for 6 to 7 hours.

HUNGARIAN GOULASH

Goulash is a scrumptious and hearty stew that centers around the flavors of beef and paprika. It is not difficult to prepare, so you may want to make a little extra so you can enjoy the leftovers. A stew like this gets better with age.

This stew calls for an unusual amount of paprika from what you normally use in recipes. You can adjust the amount if you wish, but do not be afraid to use what I have listed below. The paprika makes it really good!

Ingredients:

- 2 tablespoons coconut oil
- 1½ to 2 pounds stew beef, cubed
- 3 bell peppers, sliced
- 3 large onions, diced
- 3 garlic cloves, minced
- 10 fresh tomatoes, diced OR 2 (14.5 ounce) cans diced tomatoes
- 4 cups of beef stock is best
- 4 tablespoons paprika (yes, tablespoons!)
- 4 teaspoons caraway seeds
- 1 tablespoon sea salt
- 2 teaspoons coarse black pepper

Directions:

1. Turn your slow cooker on HIGH while you get your ingredients ready.
2. In a large frying pan on your stovetop, melt the coconut oil and then place the beef cubes, bell peppers, onions, and garlic into the pan and brown them.
3. Place the browned beef and vegetables into the slow cooker.
4. Add in the diced tomatoes and beef stock.
5. Stir in the paprika, caraway seeds, salt, and pepper.
6. Place the lid on the slow cooker and turn down to LOW for 6 to 7 hours.

SLOW AND STEADY BRAISED BEEF

This stew is one that gets better the longer you cook it. The flavors are fabulous and smells amazing while it is simmering in the slow cooker.

Ingredients:

- ◆ 2 tablespoons coconut oil
- ◆ 3 pounds stew beef
- ◆ 10 large garlic cloves, lightly crushed
- ◆ 2 onions, chopped
- ◆ 2 cups sliced carrots
- ◆ 4 sweet potatoes, peeled and cubed
- ◆ 1 (12 ounce) can tomato paste
- ◆ 5 cups beef broth
- ◆ 3 bay leaves
- ◆ 4 whole cloves OR ½ teaspoon ground cloves
- ◆ 3 cinnamon sticks
- ◆ 2 teaspoons sea salt
- ◆ 1 teaspoon coarse black pepper
- ◆ 1 cup walnut halves

Directions:

1. Turn your slow cooker on HIGH while you get your ingredients ready.
2. On the stovetop in a large frying pan, brown the stew beef until golden brown.
3. Transfer the beef to your slow cooker.
4. If needed, use a little more coconut oil and sauté the garlic cloves and onions until tender (about 5 minutes).
5. Transfer the garlic and onions to the slow cooker.
6. Add the carrots, tomato paste, broth, bay leaves, cloves, cinnamon sticks, salt, and pepper to the slow cooker.
7. Place the lid on the cooker and turn the temperature down to LOW.
8. Cook for 7 to 8 hours.
9. About 30 minutes before serving, remove the cinnamon sticks, bay leaves, and whole cloves.
10. Now add the walnuts if desired.

CURRIED BEEF STEW

This stew meat flavored with curry will reward you with some incredibly good eating. The sauce makes this so tasty you will want to savor every spoonful. You won't see any leftovers with this stew.

Ingredients:

- ♦ 2 tablespoons coconut oil
- ♦ 3 pounds beef stew meat
- ♦ 4 garlic cloves, minced
- ♦ 2 onions, diced
- ♦ 4 sweet potatoes, peeled and cubed
- ♦ 6 to 7 carrots, sliced, OR you can use parsnips
- ♦ 2 cups beef broth
- ♦ 2 tablespoons curry powder
- ♦ 1 (13.5 ounce) can coconut milk

Directions:

1. Turn your slow cooker on HIGH so it can heat up while you get your ingredients ready.
2. On your stovetop, take a large frying pan and heat up the coconut oil.
3. Place the stew beef into the frying pan and sear it until it is brown on all edges.
4. Place the browned beef into your slow cooker.
5. If necessary, place more coconut oil in your frying pan so you can sauté the garlic and onions.
6. Once the garlic and onions are tender, place them in the slow cooker.
7. Place the sweet potatoes and carrots into the slow cooker.
8. Add the beef broth.
9. Sprinkle in the curry powder.
10. Place the lid on the slow cooker and turn it down to LOW.
11. Cook for 7 to 8 hours or until the beef is really tender.
12. Just before serving, pour in the can of coconut milk and heat thoroughly.

VEGETABLE BEEF STEW

You just can't get much tastier than good ol' fashioned vegetable beef stew. This one contains some delicious mixes of spices, and the taste of the vegetables warms you down to your toenails!

Ingredients:

♦ 2 tablespoons coconut oil
♦ 3 pounds roast with the bone, meat cut into cubes
♦ 2 onions, diced
♦ 4 garlic cloves, minced
♦ 1 bag frozen okra pieces
♦ 4 tomatoes, chopped
♦ 4 carrots, sliced
♦ 4 cups chicken broth
♦ 6-ounce can tomato paste
♦ 1 tablespoon paprika
♦ 1 tablespoon sea salt
♦ 2 teaspoons coarse black pepper
♦ 1 teaspoon onion powder
♦ 2 teaspoons dried thyme
♦ 1 tablespoon oregano
♦ 1½ to 2 teaspoons cayenne pepper

Directions:

1. Turn your slow cooker on HIGH while you get your ingredients ready.
2. Place a frying pan on your stove top and heat up the coconut oil.
3. Place the roast cubes AND the bone into the frying pan and sear on all sides.
4. Place the bone and cubes into the slow cooker.
5. Return to the stove top and sauté the onions and garlic until tender.
6. Place these into the slow cooker.
7. Put the okra pieces, tomatoes, carrots, broth, and tomato sauce into the slow cooker.
8. Place the lid on the slow cooker, turn the temperature down to LOW, and cook for 8 hours.
9. About 30 minutes before serving, add all the spices and stir gently to combine.

TACO SOUP

Looking for a tasty Mexican dish that is Paleolithic? Well, try this one. The flavors are fantastic and will explode in your mouth!

With this recipe, you can either eliminate the diced tomatoes during the cooking time in the slow cooker, or add finely diced tomatoes to your soup when you serve it. And don't forget the chopped fresh cilantro and sliced avocados as a garnish, too.

Ingredients:

- 1–2 tablespoons coconut oil
- 5 garlic cloves, minced
- 2 onions, chopped
- 3 pounds ground beef
- 4 cups beef broth
- 2 (4 ounce) cans fire-roasted green chilies
- 2 cups of your favorite salsa
- 1½ tablespoons chili powder
- 6 tomatoes, diced (for the slow cooker or when serving)
- 2 teaspoons ground cumin
- 2 teaspoons sea salt
- 1 teaspoon coarse black pepper
- ½ teaspoon garlic powder
- 1 teaspoon dried oregano
- ½ teaspoon onion powder
- 1 teaspoon paprika

Directions:

1. Turn your slow cooker on HIGH while you get your ingredients ready.
2. On your stovetop, use a large frying pan to heat up the coconut oil.
3. Place the garlic and onions in the oil and sauté until tender.
4. Place the veggies in the slow cooker.
5. Brown the ground beef in the frying pan.
6. Place the browned beef into the slow cooker.
7. Add the broth, chilies, salsa, chili powder, and tomatoes if desired.
8. Cover with the lid and lower the temperature to LOW.
9. Cook for 7 to 8 hours.
10. About 30 minutes before serving, add all the spices and stir gently to combine.
11. Serve and top with your favorite garnishes.

BUTTERNUT AND PUMPKIN STEW

This beef stew is a wonderful blend of squash and pumpkin with some sweetness thrown in for flavor. Any time of year is good for enjoying stew as tasty as this.

Ingredients:

- ♦ 2 tablespoons coconut oil
- ♦ 3 pounds beef stew meat
- ♦ 2 onions, chopped
- ♦ 4 garlic cloves, minced
- ♦ 6 cups beef broth
- ♦ 3 bay leaves
- ♦ 1½ cups dried cherries
- ♦ 2–3 teaspoons sea salt
- ♦ 4 cups cubed butternut squash
- ♦ 1 teaspoon nutmeg
- ♦ 2 teaspoons allspice
- ♦ 2 teaspoons thyme
- ♦ 15 ounces canned 100% pumpkin

Directions:

1. Turn your slow cooker on HIGH while you get your ingredients ready.
2. On the stovetop, heat up the coconut oil in a large frying pan.
3. Brown the stew meat on all sides.
4. Place the meat into the slow cooker.
5. Sauté the onions and garlic until tender in the frying pan.
6. Place the onions and garlic into the slow cooker.
7. Add the broth, bay leaves, cherries, and salt.
8. Place the lid on the cooker and turn down to LOW.
9. Cook for 8 hours.
10. Approximately 2 hours before you are ready to serve the stew, add the squash, nutmeg, allspice, and thyme.
11. Continue cooking for the remaining two hours.
12. Just before serving, open the canned pumpkin and puree to a smooth consistency.
13. Add the pumpkin to the stew to help thicken.

POPEYE SOUP

This soup is a delicious combination of meat, pumpkin, and spinach and has a nice kick to it. If you do not like spicy hot soup, be sure to use a can of mild chilies instead of hot ones.

Ingredients:

- 2 tablespoons coconut oil
- 3 pounds stew meat
- 8 garlic cloves, minced
- 2 onions, chopped
- 3 pounds spinach
- 4 cups beef broth
- 4-ounce can hot green chilies
- 2 tablespoons sea salt
- 3 cups of cubed pumpkin or sweet potatoes

Directions:

1. Turn your slow cooker on HIGH while you get your ingredients ready.
2. Place the spinach leaves on the bottom of the slow cooker.
3. If desired and you have time, heat up the coconut oil in a large frying pan.
4. Add the stew meat and brown.
5. Place the stew meat on top of the spinach in the slow cooker.
6. Sauté the garlic and onions in the coconut oil until tender.
7. Transfer these to the slow cooker.
8. Add the broth, chilies, salt, and pumpkin/sweet potatoes.
9. Turn your slow cooker down to LOW and cook for 8 hours.

HEARTY GREEN SOUP

This is a soup full of goodness. Not only do you get the nutrition of the greens, but combined with the beef and vegetables, you're going to find that you like this soup more than you thought you would. Plus, there is plenty for everyone!

Ingredients:

- ♦ 4 cups mustard or turnip greens, chopped
- ♦ 2 tablespoons coconut oil
- ♦ 3 pounds stew beef
- ♦ 2 onions, chopped
- ♦ 5 garlic cloves, minced
- ♦ 2 cups sliced parsnips
- ♦ 1 cup diced turnips
- ♦ 2 cups sliced carrots
- ♦ 6 medium tomatoes, diced
- ♦ 2 cups diced sweet potatoes
- ♦ 6 cups beef broth
- ♦ 6 ounce can tomato paste
- ♦ 3 tablespoons coconut aminos
- ♦ 2 teaspoons cayenne pepper
- ♦ 1 tablespoon sea salt (more if desired)
- ♦ 2 teaspoons coarse black pepper

Directions:

1. Turn your slow cooker on HIGH while you get your ingredients ready.
2. Place the greens in the bottom of the cooker.
3. On your stovetop, heat up the coconut oil in a large frying pan.
4. Brown the stew meat on all sides.
5. Place the beef into the cooker on top of the greens.
6. Sauté the onions and garlic until tender.
7. Transfer the onions and garlic into the slow cooker.
8. Sprinkle the parsnips, turnips, carrots, tomatoes, and sweet potatoes into the slow cooker.
9. Combine the beef broth with the tomato paste and coconut aminos, then gently pour over the vegetables.
10. Add the cayenne pepper, salt, and pepper.
11. Place the lid on the cooker, lower the temperature to LOW, and cook for 8 to 9 hours.

Chicken Soups and Stews

CHICKEN AND BROCCOLI SOUP

You just cannot beat a great-tasting bowl of chicken soup. This soup is full of yummy vegetables, simmered for a long time in a chicken rub full of spices and broth. It is a very satisfying soup whenever you want to eat it.

Ingredients:

♦ 4 large chicken breasts, cut into bite-sized pieces
♦ Enough of your favorite rub to coat the chicken pieces
♦ 4 cups broccoli florets
♦ 4 carrots, sliced
♦ 6 stalks celery, sliced
♦ 16 ounces of your favorite mushrooms
♦ 2 onions, chopped
♦ 4 garlic cloves, minced
♦ 6 cups chicken broth
♦ 1 tablespoon basil
♦ 1 tablespoon oregano
♦ 2 teaspoons sea salt

Directions:

1. Turn your slow cooker on HIGH while you get your ingredients ready.
2. Take your chicken pieces and coat them with the rub of your choice.
3. Place the broccoli, carrots, celery, mushrooms, onions, and garlic into the slow cooker.
4. Top the vegetables with the coated chicken pieces.
5. Slowly pour the broth over the chicken and vegetables.
6. Add the basil, oregano, and salt.
7. Place the lid on the slow cooker and lower the temperature to LOW.
8. Cook for 7 to 8 hours.

DELICIOUS CHICKEN VEGGIE SOUP

This soup is very versatile. You can add any of your favorite vegetables to a delicious chicken base. I love soups like this that make it almost impossible to mess up. Have fun with it!

Ingredients:

- 3 cups of your favorite vegetables, cut up
- 3 sweet potatoes, cut into cubes
- 4 large chicken breasts
- 2 onions, diced
- 4 cloves garlic, minced
- 1 (15 ounce) can diced tomatoes, undrained
- 1 (15 ounce) can crushed tomatoes, undrained
- 2 teaspoons sea salt
- 2 teaspoons coarse black pepper
- 4 cups chicken broth
- 6-ounce can tomato paste
- 4 tablespoons balsamic vinegar
- 2 teaspoons dried oregano
- ¼ teaspoon red pepper flakes
- 1 teaspoon dried rosemary
- 1 teaspoon dried thyme
- 1 tablespoon dried basil

Directions:

1. Turn your slow cooker to HIGH while you get your ingredients ready.
2. Spray or apply coconut oil to the inside of your cooker.
3. Place the vegetables and sweet potatoes on the bottom of the cooker.
4. Now put in the chicken breasts, onions, garlic, both cans of tomatoes, salt, and pepper.
5. In a bowl or pitcher, mix together the chicken broth, tomato paste, and vinegar.
6. Mix these together thoroughly and then gently pour over the chicken and vegetables.
7. Place the lid on the slow cooker and cook on LOW for 7 to 8 hours.
8. Approximately 30 minutes or just before serving, add the oregano, red pepper flakes, rosemary, thyme, and basil, and stir gently to flavor the soup.

CHICKEN AND BACON STEW

Although this recipe takes a little more time and trouble than many recipes, the flavor from the bacon and the chicken pieces briefly fried in it will add some delicious depth of flavor to this stew.

Ingredients:

- ◆ 5 carrots, cut in small chunks
- ◆ 1 large butternut squash, peeled, seeded, and cut into cubes
- ◆ 2 sweet potatoes, cubed
- ◆ 4 large onions, peeled and quartered
- ◆ 1 pound bacon, cut into small pieces
- ◆ 4 shallots, peeled and diced
- ◆ 3 garlic cloves, minced
- ◆ 4 pounds of your favorite chicken pieces (leave skin on)
- ◆ 2 cups beef broth
- ◆ 2 teaspoons dried rosemary
- ◆ ¼ teaspoon turmeric
- ◆ 2 teaspoons dried cilantro

Directions:

1. Turn your slow cooker on HIGH while you get your ingredients ready.
2. Spray or apply coconut oil to the bottom and sides of your slow cooker.
3. Place the carrot chunks, squash, sweet potatoes, and onions in the bottom of your slow cooker.
4. On the stovetop, use a large frying pan and place the bacon pieces in it.
5. After a few minutes, add the diced shallots and garlic cloves.
6. When the bacon is done and the shallots are tender, remove from the frying pan and place in the slow cooker.
7. Slowly add your chicken pieces and cook until the skin begins to become crispy. If you need extra oil, add some coconut oil for frying.
8. Once you are pleased with the crispiness of the chicken pieces, place them into the slow cooker on top of the vegetables.
9. Pour the bacon grease into your slow cooker and be sure to scrape the sides and bottom of the pan, too.
10. Pour the broth over the chicken and vegetables.
11. You can add the rosemary, turmeric, and cilantro now, or you can wait until about 30 minutes before serving to add them.
12. Turn your slow cooker down to LOW and cook for 8 to 9 hours.

CASHEW SOUP WITH GREENS

Trust me. This soup is terrific and very versatile. You can use mustard greens, turnip greens, kale, or a combination of all these. Plus, the addition of cashews gives this soup a nice little bit of crunch.

Ingredients:

- 1 large bunch of mustard greens, turnip greens, kale, or a combination—stemmed and torn into pieces
- 4 zucchini or yellow squash, cut into chunks
- 2 tablespoons coconut oil
- 3 onions, chopped
- 4 garlic cloves, minced
- ½ teaspoon cayenne pepper
- 2 teaspoons ground ginger
- 5 chicken breasts, sliced
- 6 cups chicken broth
- 1 cup cashew butter
- 15-ounce can fire-roasted diced tomatoes
- 1 tablespoon sea salt
- 2 teaspoons coarse black pepper
- Chopped cashews (optional)

Directions:

1. Turn your slow cooker on HIGH so it can heat up as you get your ingredients ready.
2. Spray or apply coconut oil to your slow cooker insert.
3. Place the greens and zucchini on the bottom of the slow cooker.
4. On your stovetop, take a large frying pan and heat the coconut oil.
5. Place the onions in the frying pan and sauté for several minutes.
6. Add the garlic, cayenne pepper, and ginger to the frying pan.
7. After a couple of minutes, add the chicken slices and cook until browned.
8. Transfer the chicken and spices to the slow cooker and place on top of the vegetables.
9. In a separate bowl, mix the broth, cashew butter, tomatoes, salt, and pepper together.
10. Carefully pour the broth mixture over the chicken and the vegetables.
11. Turn your slow cooker down to LOW and cook for 7 to 8 hours.
12. Serve and garnish with chopped cashews sprinkled on top.

MEATY TOMATO SOUP

Tomato soup is a classic and this is no exception, except it has a twist. It packs some valuable protein because of some chicken while having a smooth texture with the addition of coconut milk.

Just toss everything into your slow cooker and enjoy the wonderful tastes at dinner or whenever!

Ingredients:

- ♦ 4 bell peppers, sliced
- ♦ 2 onions, chopped
- ♦ 4 garlic cloves, minced
- ♦ 6 boneless chicken breasts, sliced
- ♦ 2 (28 ounce) cans diced tomatoes, undrained
- ♦ 3 cups chicken broth
- ♦ 2 tablespoons dried oregano
- ♦ 2 tablespoons dried basil
- ♦ 2 teaspoons sea salt
- ♦ 2 teaspoons coarse black pepper
- ♦ 2 (14 ounce) cans coconut milk

Directions:

1. Turn your slow cooker on HIGH while you get your ingredients ready.
2. Spray or apply coconut oil to your slow cooker insert to help with sticking.
3. Put the bell peppers, onions, and garlic on the bottom of your slow cooker.
4. Put the chicken slices on top of the vegetables.
5. Pour the tomatoes and chicken broth in next.
6. Add the spices.
7. Turn the slow cooker down to LOW and cook for 8 to 9 hours.
8. About 30 minutes before serving, add the cans of coconut milk and heat through.

CURRIED CHICKEN SOUP

This recipe is especially good around the holidays when you usually have leftovers from your Thanksgiving turkey. However, if you want to make it any time of the year (like me), then chicken is a very convenient option. The Thai curry paste gives this soup a totally different flair.

Ingredients:

- 4 carrots, sliced
- 4 cups fresh green beans
- 2 large parsnips, diced
- 2 onions, chopped
- 5 garlic cloves, finely minced
- 4 cups cooked chicken or turkey, cubed
- 3 tablespoons red Thai curry paste (I use the one from Trader Joe's)
- 2 teaspoons sea salt
- 2 teaspoons coarse black pepper
- 6 cups chicken broth
- 2 (14.5 ounce) cans coconut milk

Directions:

1. Turn your slow cooker on HIGH while you get your ingredients ready.
2. Spray or apply coconut oil to the slow cooker insert.
3. Place the carrots, green beans, parsnips, onions, garlic, and cooked chicken into the slow cooker.
4. Put the curry paste, salt, and pepper in with the broth and stir to blend.
5. Pour the broth over the chicken and vegetables.
6. Turn the slow cooker down to LOW and cook for 8 hours.
7. About 30 minutes before serving, stir in the coconut milk and heat completely.

SOUTH OF THE BORDER STEW

This flavorful stew will have you thinking you crossed the border as you enjoy its spicy taste. If you think there might be too much spice, you can always tone it down with your choice of green chilies and the amount of chili powder you use.

Ingredients:

- 3 pounds chicken breasts, sliced or cubed
- 3 bell peppers, chopped
- 2 onions, chopped
- 5 garlic cloves, minced
- 2 (4 ounce) cans of green chilies (your choice of intensity)
- 28-ounce can diced tomatoes, undrained
- 2 cans Ro-tel tomato sauce
- 1 tablespoon dried oregano
- 1 tablespoon chili powder
- 1 tablespoon cumin
- 1 tablespoon dried cilantro
- 2 teaspoons sea salt
- 2 teaspoons coarse black pepper
- Fresh avocado slices for garnish (optional)

Directions:

1. Turn your slow cooker on HIGH while you get your ingredients ready.
2. Spray or apply coconut oil to your slow cooker insert.
3. Place your chicken pieces into the slow cooker.
4. Add the peppers, onions, garlic, chilies, tomatoes, tomato sauce, and all the spices into the slow cooker.
5. Place the lid on the top and lower the temperature to LOW.
6. Cook for 8 hours.
7. Garnish with avocado if desired.

GOOD OL' CHICKEN SOUP

There are so many wonderful flavors you can add to a basic and delicious chicken soup. This one has some healthy vegetables you can bite into, along with a little kick, compliments of the chili powder.

Ingredients:

- ◆   3 cups fresh green beans
- ◆   4 cups sliced carrots
- ◆   3 zucchinis, diced
- ◆   3 yellow squash, diced
- ◆   4–5 cups cooked chicken or turkey
- ◆   3 onions, chopped
- ◆   5 garlic cloves, minced
- ◆   8 cups chicken broth
- ◆   1 tablespoon Italian seasonings
- ◆   1 tablespoon sea salt
- ◆   2 teaspoons coarse black pepper
- ◆   2 teaspoons chili powder

Directions:

1. Turn your slow cooker on HIGH while you get your ingredients ready.
2. Spray or apply coconut oil to your slow cooker insert.
3. In the bottom of the slow cooker, place the green beans, carrots, zucchini, squash, cooked chicken, onions, and garlic.
4. Pour the chicken broth over the chicken and vegetables.
5. Add the Italian seasoning, salt, pepper, and chili powder.
6. Place the cover on the slow cooker and set the temperature to LOW.
7. Cook for 6 to 7 hours.

CHICKEN AND RICE SOUP

One of the challenges of living a Paleolithic lifestyle is finding substitutes for things like pasta and rice. Many know that cauliflower works as a substitute, and this recipe is no exception. However, the best part is you do not even have to cook the cauliflower!

Ingredients:

♦ 2½ to 3 pounds chicken breast, sliced into strips
♦ 4 garlic cloves, minced
♦ 2 onions, chopped
♦ 1 (14 ounce) jar of roasted red peppers
♦ 2 (14 ounce) cans diced tomatoes, undrained
♦ 1½ cups chicken broth
♦ 1½ tablespoons chili powder
♦ 2 teaspoons garlic powder
♦ 2 teaspoons dried oregano
♦ 4 teaspoons cumin powder
♦ 2 teaspoons sea salt
♦ 2 teaspoons coarse black pepper
♦ 1 large head cauliflower
♦ 1 bunch fresh cilantro (enough for 4 tablespoons)

Directions:

1. Turn your slow cooker on HIGH while you get your ingredients ready.
2. Spray or apply some coconut oil to your slow cooker insert.
3. Place the chicken slices, garlic, onions, and peppers in the bottom of the slow cooker.
4. Gently pour in the diced tomatoes and chicken broth.
5. Add the chili powder, garlic powder, oregano, cumin, salt, and pepper.
6. Cover with the lid and turn the slow cooker down to LOW.
7. Cook for 6 hours.
8. Several minutes before you want to serve the chicken, pulse the cauliflower in a food processor until you have the consistency of "rice."
9. Empty the cauliflower into a serving bowl and mix in the fresh cilantro.
10. When ready to serve, place some "rice" in the bottom of a soup bowl and cover with the chicken.

Pork Soups and Stews

PORK STEW WITH A KICK

Pork is delicious as a protein, and this stew is no exception. Be sure to cook it long enough so it has time to get tender. Then, when you come to the "kick" part of this recipe, decide if you want a lot of kick or a milder one, and select the heat intensity of the green chilies.

Ingredients:

- 2 tablespoons coconut oil
- 2 bell peppers, diced
- 2 large onions, chopped
- 4 garlic cloves, minced
- 3 pounds pork, cut into trimmed cubes
- 2 cups chicken broth
- 2 teaspoons sea salt
- 2 teaspoons coarse black pepper
- 1 tablespoon ground cumin
- 1 tablespoon dried oregano
- 3 (14.5 ounce) cans Ro-tel tomatoes with mild green chilies
- 1 (4 ounce) can diced green chilies (you decide how hot)
- 3 tablespoons lime juice

Directions:

1. Turn your slow cooker on HIGH while you get your ingredients ready.
2. Spray or apply some coconut oil to the insert of your slow cooker.
3. On the stovetop, heat the coconut oil in a large frying pan.
4. Sauté the bell peppers, onions, and garlic until tender.
5. Add these to the slow cooker.
6. If necessary, add a little more coconut oil so you can brown the pork cubes until they are browned on all sides.
7. Add these to the slow cooker as well.
8. Add some of the chicken broth to your frying pan and scrape the sides to loosen any of the pork and veggies left behind.
9. Add this broth to the slow cooker, along with the remaining broth.
10. Season the pork with the salt, pepper, cumin, and oregano.
11. Pour the entire contents of the cans of tomatoes into the slow cooker over the chicken.
12. Finish by adding the can of chilies and lime juice.
13. Place the cover on the slow cooker and turn the temperature down to LOW.
14. Cook for 7 to 8 hours.
15. Serve and garnish with your favorite topping.

PORK AND SWEET POTATO SOUP

Pork and sweet potatoes go well together as an entrée and side dish, and as a soup featuring both these ingredients, it is a winning combination. Try this one and see what you and your crew think.

Ingredients:

- ♦ 4 sweet potatoes, peeled and cut into cubes
- ♦ 4 stalks celery, sliced
- ♦ 2 onions, chopped
- ♦ 4 garlic cloves, minced
- ♦ 3 cups cooked pork, cubed or shredded
- ♦ 4 cups chicken broth
- ♦ 1 tablespoon sea salt
- ♦ 2 teaspoons coarse black pepper
- ♦ 3 (13.5 ounce) cans coconut milk

Directions:

1. Turn your slow cooker on HIGH while you get your ingredients ready.
2. Spray or apply coconut oil to the insert of your slow cooker.
3. Place the sweet potatoes, celery, onions, and garlic in the bottom of your slow cooker.
4. Now add the pork.
5. Pour in the chicken broth and add the salt and pepper.
6. Turn your slow cooker down to LOW and cook for 5 to 6 hours.
7. About 30 minutes before you want to serve it, pour in the coconut milk and heat thoroughly.

APPLE AND SWEET POTATO STEW

My daughter likes to say, "Fall just smells good." I have to agree. When the weather begins to cool off, the air smells crisper and lifts my spirits.

Well, here is a stew that "smells good." Yes, it tastes good, too. Try this enjoyable combination of sweet apple flavor with your pork and potatoes. Enjoy!

Ingredients:

- ♦ 2 large tart apples, peeled and chopped
- ♦ 3 sweet potatoes, peeled and cubed
- ♦ 2 onions, chopped
- ♦ 4 celery stalks, sliced
- ♦ 4 garlic cloves, minced
- ♦ 2 pounds pork meat, cut into cubes or slices
- ♦ 3 cups chicken broth
- ♦ 3 cups apple cider OR more chicken broth
- ♦ 2 tablespoons poultry seasoning, or see next page
- ♦ 1 teaspoon sea salt
- ♦ 1 teaspoon coarse black pepper
- ♦ 2 tablespoons apple cider vinegar
- ♦ 2 teaspoons vanilla extract
- ♦ 2 teaspoons pumpkin pie spice blend, or see next page

If you do not have pumpkin pie spice, you can make your own:

- ¼ teaspoon ground cloves
- 1 teaspoon ground cinnamon
- ¼ teaspoon ground allspice
- ¼ teaspoon ground ginger
- ¼ teaspoon ground nutmeg

If you do not have poultry seasoning, you can make your own:

- 1½ teaspoons ground thyme
- 2 teaspoons ground sage
- 1 teaspoon ground marjoram
- ½ teaspoon nutmeg
- ¾ teaspoon ground rosemary
- ½ teaspoon coarse black pepper

Directions:

1. Turn your slow cooker on HIGH while you get your ingredients ready.
2. Spray or apply coconut oil to the insert of your slow cooker.
3. Place the apple pieces and sweet potatoes in the bottom of your slow cooker.
4. Now put in the onions, celery, and garlic.
5. Pour the chicken broth and cider into the slow cooker.
6. Add the spices.
7. Turn your slow cooker down to LOW and cook for 7 to 8 hours.
8. About 30 minutes before you serve the stew, add the cider vinegar and vanilla.

INDIAN PORK AND SQUASH STEW

Pork and squash make a tasty combination when you cook them together in your slow cooker. I like to use garam masala as an ingredient. Garam masala is blend of ground spices common in North India. If you do not have any, you can make your own using the following amounts and ingredients, then store in an airtight container so you have some the next time you make this recipe.

Make your own garam masala:

- 1 teaspoon ground cloves
- 1 tablespoon ground coriander
- 1 teaspoon ground nutmeg
- 2 teaspoons ground cinnamon
- 2 tablespoons ground cumin
- 1 tablespoon ground pepper
- 1 tablespoon ground cardamom

Mix all of these together and store in an airtight container. Now you have some garam masala to use in this dish!

Ingredients for stew:

- 1 bunch kale, stemmed and shredded
- 4 carrots, sliced
- 2 tart apples, peeled and chopped
- 1 pound butternut squash, peeled, seeded, and cubed
- 4 celery stalks, chopped
- 2 tablespoons coconut oil
- 3 pounds pork, cubed
- 3 onions, chopped

- 6 garlic cloves, minced
- 1 tablespoon garam masala
- 2 teaspoons sea salt
- 1 tablespoon lemon juice
- 2 cups chicken broth
- ½ cup unsweetened coconut milk

Directions:

1. Turn your slow cooker on HIGH while you get your ingredients ready.
2. Spray or apply coconut oil to the insert of your slow cooker.
3. Place the kale in the bottom of the slow cooker.
4. Now add the carrots, apples, squash, and celery.
5. On the stovetop, use a large frying pan to heat up the coconut oil.
6. Brown the pork cubes until they are slightly crunchy looking.
7. Transfer to your slow cooker.
8. Return to your frying pan and sauté the onions and garlic until tender.
9. Add these to your slow cooker.
10. Sprinkle the garam masala over the pork.
11. Add the salt, lemon juice, and broth.
12. Cover the slow cooker with the lid and lower the temperature to LOW.
13. Cook for 7 to 8 hours.
14. About 30 minutes before serving, add the coconut milk and heat through.

ITALIAN SOUP

One of the comments I hear a lot from people who are enjoying a Paleolithic lifestyle is how they occasionally miss eating pasta dishes and foods with a crust. I have to admit that I do as well on occasion.

In an effort to enjoy a favorite dish in a completely new way, I created this soup full of goodies you would normally find in an Italian restaurant, but there is not any crust to this one. Try it and I think you will enjoy the results as much as I do.

Ingredients:

- 2 pounds ground beef
- 2 pounds sausage
- 2 onions, chopped
- 4 garlic cloves, minced
- 4 bell peppers, diced
- 2 cups mushrooms, sliced
- 2 cups tomatoes, diced
- 1 (28 ounce) can tomato sauce
- 2 (6 ounce) cans tomato paste
- 6 cups chicken broth
- 4 tablespoons dried oregano
- 1 tablespoon dried basil
- 1 tablespoon paprika

Garnish with your favorite toppings, like:

◆ Black olives

◆ Bacon bits

◆ Crushed red peppers

◆ Favorite shredded aged cheese (if you eat dairy products)

◆ Artichokes

◆ Pineapple

Directions:

1. Turn your slow cooker on HIGH while you get your ingredients ready.
2. Spray or apply coconut oil to your insert to keep it from sticking.
3. On your stovetop, use a large frying pan to brown the ground beef and sausage (do 2 batches if your pan isn't big enough to handle both).
4. Place the browned meat into the slow cooker.
5. Add your onions, garlic, bell peppers, mushrooms, and tomatoes.
6. Pour in the tomato sauce.
7. In a large bowl, mix the tomato paste with the chicken broth, then add to the slow cooker.
8. Turn your slow cooker down to LOW and cook for 6 to 7 hours.
9. A few minutes before serving, add the oregano, basil, and paprika, and stir in.
10. Serve the soup when ready and garnish with your favorite toppings.

SAUSAGE AND APPLE STEW

Sometimes it is just fun to do something a little different, and this stew does just that. With sausage as the main meat and the addition of apples and raisins, you have yourself a pot full of goodness and fun—not to mention they taste great together.

Ingredients:

- ♦ 6 carrots, sliced
- ♦ 4 sweet potatoes, peeled and diced
- ♦ 3 tart apples, peeled and diced
- ♦ 6 celery stalks, chopped or sliced
- ♦ 2 tablespoons coconut oil
- ♦ 3 onions, chopped
- ♦ 4 garlic cloves, minced
- ♦ 3 pounds sausage
- ♦ 4 cups chicken broth
- ♦ ¼ cup raw honey (optional)
- ♦ ¼ cup balsamic vinegar
- ♦ ¼ cup spicy mustard
- ♦ 2 teaspoons sea salt
- ♦ 1 teaspoon black pepper
- ♦ 1 cup raisins
- ♦ 1 teaspoon ground allspice

Directions:

1. Turn your slow cooker on HIGH while you get your ingredients ready.
2. Spray or apply coconut oil to the insert of your slow cooker.
3. Place the carrots, sweet potatoes, apples, and celery on the bottom of the slow cooker.
4. On your stovetop, heat up the coconut oil in a large frying pan.
5. Sauté the onions and garlic for about 5 minutes so they can get tender, then put them in the slow cooker.
6. Brown the sausage and then drain it.
7. Put it into the slow cooker.
8. In a separate bowl, stir together the chicken broth, honey, balsamic vinegar, and mustard.
9. Add this liquid to the sausage and vegetables.
10. Add salt and pepper.
11. Place the lid on your slow cooker and turn the temperature down to LOW
12. Cook for 7 to 8 hours.
13. About 30 minutes before serving, add the raisins and allspice.

Seafood Soups and Stews

CRAB STEW WITH VEGETABLES

I am a huge fan of seafood, and crab is one of my favorites. Growing up on the water, I remember days when we would catch crabs using a rope with a chicken neck tied to the end. The crab would grab ahold of the neck, and then we would come up behind them with a net and snag them. So easy!

After we caught a bunch of them, we would steam them, spread out the newspaper on the tables, and pick and eat crab until our tummies ran out of room. Ahhh! Sweet memories.

If you live on the water and have access to live crabs, you can make this stew fresher than most, or save yourself the trouble and buy the lump crabmeat already picked. This is not a cheap stew by any means, but it is oh, so delicious!

Ingredients:

- 4 cups parsnips, peeled and diced (about 2 pounds)
- 4 cups frozen green beans
- 4 carrots, sliced
- 3 onions, chopped
- 4 garlic cloves, minced
- 4 celery stalks, chopped
- 1 large can diced tomatoes, undrained
- 6 cups chicken broth
- 4 bay leaves
- 2–3 tablespoons Old Bay seasoning (it is gluten-free)
- 1 tablespoon dried thyme
- 2 teaspoons sea salt
- 2 teaspoons coarse black pepper
- 3 pounds crabmeat
- ¼ cup fresh parsley, finely chopped

Directions:

1. Turn your slow cooker on HIGH while you get your ingredients ready.
2. Spray or apply coconut oil to the insert of your slow cooker.
3. Place the parsnips, green beans, carrots, onions, garlic, and celery into the slow cooker.
4. Now pour in the diced tomatoes and chicken broth.
5. Add the bay leaves, Old Bay, thyme, salt, and pepper.
6. Cover with the lid and turn the slow cooker down to LOW.
7. Cook for 6 to 7 hours.
8. About 45 minutes to 1 hour before serving, add the crabmeat and parsley.

JAMBALAYA

Jambalaya is one of our family's favorite soups. Depending upon the age and tastes of your diners, you may want to cut back on some of the spiciness of this dish. Since eating Paleolithic, I have found I enjoy foods spicier than I used to; however, I still do not like my nose to run faster than I do! Enjoy.

Ingredients:

- 4 bell peppers, chopped
- 2 large onions, chopped
- 4 celery stalks, sliced
- 4 cloves garlic, minced
- 4 bay leaves
- 2 large cans diced tomatoes, undrained
- 3–4 cups chicken, cubed
- 6 cups chicken broth
- ¼–⅓ cup your favorite hot sauce (I like Frank's hot sauce)
- 2 pounds frozen shrimp, thawed
- 12 ounce package Andouille sausage
- 3 cups okra
- ⅛–¼ cup Cajun seasoning, or see below
- 1 head cauliflower

Recipe to make your own Cajun seasoning:
- 1 tablespoon coarse black pepper
- 1 tablespoon dried oregano
- 1 tablespoon paprika
- 2½ tablespoons sea salt
- 1 tablespoon cayenne pepper

Directions:

1. Turn your slow cooker on HIGH while you get your ingredients ready.
2. Spray or apply coconut oil to the insert of your slow cooker.
3. Place the bell peppers, onions, celery, garlic, and bay leaves into the slow cooker.
4. Pour the diced tomatoes over the vegetables.
5. Add the chicken cubes, chicken broth, and hot sauce.
6. Cover with the lid, turn the slow cooker down to LOW, and cook for 6 hours.
7. At 30 minutes before serving, add the shrimp, sausage, okra, and seasonings.
8. Allow them to cook until the shrimp is pink and the okra is cooked.
9. At this point, you can pulse the head of cauliflower in your food processor to create "rice." Then you can add it to your slow cooker OR use it to go under the jambalaya when you serve it.

FISH SOUP

I have to admit that I am not much of a fish lover, but I found that I really enjoy fish when I put it in this soup. I use a mild-tasting fish, and the vegetables make it a hearty and satisfying meal. Feel free to spice it up more if you like.

Ingredients:

♦ 2 pounds parsnips, peeled and diced

♦ 4 celery stalks, sliced

♦ 4 carrots, sliced or diced

♦ 4 cups green beans

♦ ½ pound bacon, sliced

♦ 2 onions, diced

♦ 4 garlic cloves, minced

♦ 2½–3 pounds fish fillets, chunked

♦ 6 cups chicken broth

♦ 4 bay leaves

♦ 2 tablespoons homemade Worcestershire sauce (see below)

♦ 2 tablespoons Old Bay seasoning (you can use your favorite spicy seasoning here if you wish)

♦ 2 (13.5 ounce) cans coconut milk

Directions:

1. Turn your slow cooker to HIGH while you get your ingredients ready.
2. Spray or apply coconut oil to the insert of your slow cooker.
3. Place the parsnips, carrots, celery, and green beans into the bottom of the slow cooker.
4. On your stovetop, use a large frying pan and cook the bacon.
5. A few minutes into frying the bacon, add the onions and garlic.
6. Once the bacon has finished cooking, add to the slow cooker.
7. Add the fish, chicken broth, bay leaves, Worcestershire sauce, and Old Bay.

8. Put the lid on the slow cooker, lower the temperature to LOW, and cook for 6 hours.
9. About 30 minutes before serving, add the coconut milk.
10. Heat thoroughly, then serve.

Homemade Worcestershire sauce:

Here is a Paleolithic-friendly condiment you can make yourself and keep on hand whenever you find a recipe you want to convert to Paleolithic.

♦   1 cup apple cider vinegar
♦   ¼ cup coconut aminos
♦   ¼ cup Thai fish sauce (optional, but makes it taste great)
♦   ¼ cup water
♦   ¼ teaspoon coarse black pepper
♦   ½ teaspoon dry mustard
♦   ½ teaspoon onion powder
♦   ¼ teaspoon ground cinnamon
♦   ½ teaspoon ground ginger
♦   ½ teaspoon garlic powder

1. Place all the ingredients into a saucepan on your stovetop
2. Bring to a boil and allow it to simmer for 1 to 2 minutes
3. Cool and store in a container in your refrigerator

SEAFOOD AND CHICKEN STEW

Here is a tasty combination of shrimp, clams, and chicken that will satisfy even the hungriest members in your family. It is a very versatile recipe as well. You can eliminate the tomatoes if you like and add coconut milk near the end of cooking to get more of a "New England" style stew. Additionally, you can add in scallops or crabs if you like. Just have fun with it. It will taste great no matter what you do to it.

Ingredients:

- 2 onions, diced
- 4 stalks celery, chopped
- 4 bell peppers, diced
- 4 garlic cloves, minced
- 1 small can green chilies (your choice of intensity)
- 1 pound chicken, cubed or sliced
- 4 cups chicken broth
- 2 (15 ounce) cans clam stock or broth
- 1 (6 ounce) can tomato paste
- 2 (14.5 ounce) cans diced tomatoes
- 2 teaspoons sea salt
- 1 teaspoon coarse black pepper
- 2 teaspoons chili powder
- ½ teaspoon cayenne pepper
- 1 pound whitefish fillets, cubed
- 2 pounds medium shrimp, fresh or thawed if frozen
- 2 (10 ounce) cans clams, drained
- 2 teaspoons dried oregano
- ½ cup fresh parsley, chopped
- Your favorite hot sauce

Directions:

1. Turn your slow cooker on HIGH so it can heat up while you get your ingredients ready.
2. Spray or apply coconut oil to the insert of your slow cooker.
3. Add all the ingredients down through the cayenne pepper to your slow cooker.
4. Place the lid on and lower the temperature to LOW.
5. Cook for 6 hours.
6. About 1 hour before serving, add the fish, shrimp, clams, and oregano.
7. Cook until shrimp and fish are done.
8. Garnish with fresh parsley and a dash (or two) of your favorite hot sauce.

Vegetable Soups and Stews

BUTTERNUT SQUASH SOUP

Here is a nice, smooth soup that goes down with a smile on your face. You will like the combination of squash and apples. Plus, this recipe lends itself to adding a protein if you wish.

Ingredients:

- ♦ 1 large butternut squash, peeled and cubed
- ♦ 3 large tart apples, peeled and cubed
- ♦ 4 celery stalks, chopped
- ♦ 4 garlic cloves, minced
- ♦ 2 onions, chopped
- ♦ 6 cups chicken broth
- ♦ 1½ tablespoons ground ginger
- ♦ 2 teaspoons curry powder
- ♦ ½ teaspoon ground nutmeg
- ♦ 1 teaspoon ground cinnamon
- ♦ 2 teaspoons sea salt
- ♦ 1 teaspoon coarse black pepper
- ♦ 2 (14.5 ounce) cans coconut milk

Directions:

1. Turn your slow cooker on HIGH while you get your ingredients ready.
2. Spray or apply coconut oil to the insert of your slow cooker.
3. Place the squash, apples, celery, garlic, onions, and chicken broth in the slow cooker.
4. Add the ginger, curry, nutmeg, cinnamon, salt, and pepper.
5. Place the lid on the slow cooker and lower the temperature to LOW.
6. Cook for 7 to 8 hours.

7. About 30 minutes before serving, take an immersion blender and blend the ingredients until the soup is the consistency you desire (or process in batches in a blender).
8. Add the coconut milk and heat through.
9. Garnish as desired.

FRENCH ONION AND MUSHROOM SOUP

One of my favorite soups is French Onion; however, when you eat Paleolithic style, you don't want the slice of bread on the bottom. Here is my variation of this classic soup.

Ingredients:

- ♦ 6 large onions, chopped
- ♦ 3 (16 ounce) packages of mushrooms (use a combination of different kinds if you like)
- ♦ 4 garlic cloves, minced
- ♦ 4 cups chicken broth
- ♦ 4 cups beef or vegetable broth
- ♦ ¼ cup coconut oil (optional, but good)
- ♦ 2 teaspoons homemade Worcestershire sauce
- ♦ 1 tablespoon sea salt
- ♦ 2 teaspoons coarse black pepper
- ♦ ¼ teaspoon thyme

Directions:

1. Turn your slow cooker on HIGH while you get your ingredients ready.
2. Spray or apply coconut oil to the insert of your slow cooker.
3. Place the onions, mushrooms, garlic, and broths in the slow cooker.
4. Add the coconut oil if desired, along with the Worcestershire sauce, salt, and pepper.
5. Cover and lower the temperature down to LOW.
6. Cook for 7 to 8 hours.
7. Before serving, take an immersion blender and blend the soup mixture until desired consistency.
8. Stir in the thyme.
9. If you eat dairy, you can sprinkle with shredded aged cheeses of your choice when you serve it up.

CURRIED APPLE AND POTATO SOUP

If you enjoy the taste of curry, this soup will fill your heart with happiness. Using a combination of sweet potatoes, apples, and curry powder, this soup not only tastes good, but also smells terrific while it is cooking. Your crew, and you, will be excited when it is time to eat this one.

Ingredients:

- ◆ 4 large sweet potatoes, peeled and cut into chunks
- ◆ 2 large onions, diced
- ◆ 4 garlic cloves, minced
- ◆ 4 celery stalks, chopped
- ◆ 3 large apples, peeled and diced
- ◆ 6 cups chicken broth
- ◆ 2 teaspoons sea salt
- ◆ 2 teaspoons coarse black pepper
- ◆ 2 tablespoons curry powder
- ◆ 2 tablespoons ground ginger
- ◆ 1 teaspoon ground nutmeg
- ◆ 2 teaspoons ground cinnamon
- ◆ 1½ tablespoons lime juice
- ◆ 2 (14.5 ounce) cans coconut milk
- ◆ ¼ cup fresh cilantro, chopped (for a garnish)

Directions:

1. Turn your slow cooker on HIGH while you get your ingredients ready.
2. Spray or apply coconut oil to the inside of your insert.
3. Place the potatoes, onions, garlic, celery, apples, broth, salt, pepper, and ginger in the slow cooker.
4. Cover and turn the temperature down to LOW.
5. Cook for 6 to 7 hours.
6. About 30 minutes before time to eat, take an immersion blender and blend to your desired consistency (or process the soup in your blender in batches).
7. Now add the nutmeg, cinnamon, lime juice, and coconut milk, and heat thoroughly.
8. Serve and sprinkle with cilantro.

Quick Breads and Muffins

FABULOUS PALEOLITHIC QUICK BREADS

If you are like me, one of the things you really enjoy with your soup or stew is a pumpkin muffin or a slice of banana bread. A nice hot muffin straight out of the oven is a perfect match for a hot and hearty meal.

Below I have included information on how to cook quick breads in your slow cooker, just in case you do not want to heat up your kitchen and you would like to save a little money by using your slow cooker instead of your oven.

While all the recipes in this section are written as if you were **cooking muffins in the oven in muffin tins**, which takes about 15 to 18 minutes, I have had great success making sweet breads in bread-loaf pans in my oven AND slow cooker. When I cook them in the oven, it takes about 30 to 35 minutes. When I cook them in my slow cooker, it takes approximately 2 hours when my slow cooker is set on HIGH.

When you are cooking a loaf of bread in your slow cooker, you have to keep an eye on your loaf near the end of the 2 hours to make sure it does not burn and to make sure the loaf is thoroughly cooked in the middle. Just test it with a toothpick or cake tester to make sure it comes out clean. Sometimes I have to cook it an additional 10 to 15 minutes to get the middle thoroughly cooked.

Whichever way you decide to cook the following recipes, you will enjoy their flavor and texture. **The fact that they are Paleolithic AND gluten free is an added bonus!**

The next section will explain how you cook quick (or sweet) breads in your slow cooker if you decide to do this instead of in your oven.

SLOW COOKER QUICK BREADS

S o, I bet you are wondering how in the world you can cook quick bread in your slow cooker; that is unless you've read my other slow cooker book entitled, *Paleolithic Slow Cooker: Simple & Healthy Gluten-Free Recipes* where I told you how. While I know quick breads are not usually cooked in a slow cooker, there are times when you might want to do this because of time issues, because you are trying to save a little money, or just because *you can!* I find it is a fun way to **wow** my friends when I tell them I can do this.

In the recipes that follow, most have some type of sweetener in them. Sweeteners are optional and have not seemed to affect the texture very much. You will just have to decide if you want the little bit added in or not. If you are like me, you seldom even eat muffins or breads, so when you do, it falls well within Mark Sisson's 80/20 rule (eat Paleolithic 80 percent of the time and have a little fun the other 20 percent).

This next section includes numerous recipes that have become some of my favorites and can be cooked in your slow cooker in a bread loaf pan. **Please note: you will need to use a 6-quart oblong slow cooker in order to fit most bread pans inside.**

Before you do so, I want to walk you through the process so you will know how to do this. Once you learn it, you can make just about any loaf of sweet bread you want. Remember, just take any regular muffin recipe, put it into your bread pan, then cook in your slow cooker. The possibilities are endless!

1. Because regular muffin pans will not fit inside a slow cooker, you will have to cook these recipes in a loaf pan that fits inside your slow cooker. **Be sure to test to see if your loaf pan fits inside your slow cooker before you start!** Most 6-quart oblong slow cookers will hold a regular bread pan (8½ x 4½).

2. You will want to form four small balls made out of foil to elevate your loaf pan off the bottom of your slow cooker. If you have a small rack that fits in the bottom of your slow cooker, you can use that instead.

3. Be sure to spray your loaf pan with coconut oil spray or grease it with coconut oil. Coconut oil can withstand high temperatures and will not burn.

4. Once you treat your bread pan, place it down into the slow cooker, on top of the foil balls, and turn the slow cooker on and up to HIGH. This will allow it to preheat—just like you do your oven. If you wish, you can place your loaf pan down into the slow cooker, onto the foil balls, before you fill it with the batter or wait until the pan is filled. Be sure to use hand protection if you wait until after it is filled so you do not burn yourself by touching the sides of the slow cooker.

5. While each slow cooker is different, it will take about 2 hours for your loaf to cook completely. Test the center for doneness using a toothpick or cake tester.

6. When cooking these recipes, be sure you turn the lid slightly crooked so steam can escape, or prop your lid open with a couple of toothpicks. You do not want the condensation that normally forms on the lid to fall into your loaf.

7. Once your loaf is thoroughly cooked, allow it to sit in the pan for 15 minutes, and then carefully dump it out onto a cooling rack.

8. Once it is thoroughly cooled, which takes about another 30 minutes to an hour, you can slice yourself a piece and feast on the flavor. (Can you tell I like nuts?) And by the way, grass-fed butter is optional.

Let this be the start of some wonderful baking at your house as you experiment and try new Paleolithic breads in your slow cooker!

So, without any further ado, I present to you Paleolithic quick breads and muffins!

PUMPKIN BREAD

Pumpkin bread is a delicious addition to any meal, especially during the fall and winter when you can't help but think about the holidays.

This bread is also a healthy snack when you just want a little something with your coffee or tea in the afternoon. Hope you enjoy it as much as our family does.

Ingredients:

- ¾ cup canned pumpkin
- ¼ cup raw honey or pure maple syrup (you can use less or eliminate)
- 1 tablespoon almond butter
- 3 large eggs
- 1½ cups almond flour
- 1 teaspoon ground cinnamon
- 1 teaspoon baking soda
- 1 teaspoon baking powder
- 1 tablespoon pumpkin pie spice
- ½ teaspoon sea salt

Directions:

1. Turn on your slow cooker to HIGH while you get your ingredients ready.
2. Spray or apply coconut oil to the sides and bottom of your loaf pan.
3. In a blender, place the pumpkin, honey, almond butter, and eggs.
4. Turn blender on low and allow it to run while you mix the dry ingredients together in a separate mixing bowl.
5. Once the dry ingredients are blended together, slowly pour the pumpkin mixture into the dry ingredients and blend until mixed completely.
6. Pour the batter into the loaf pan.
7. Place the lid on your slow cooker, using a couple of toothpicks to prop it up to reduce any condensation.
8. Cook on HIGH for 2 hours.
9. Using a toothpick, check for doneness.
10. Remove from the slow cooker and place the pan on a cooling rack for 15 minutes.
11. Using a knife, scrape the sides loose and gently invert the bread pan so the loaf is on the cooling rack.
12. Allow to cool completely.
13. Slice and butter if desired.

BANANA WALNUT BREAD

Ingredients:

- ◆ 3 ripe bananas
- ◆ 3 eggs (bring to room temperature)
- ◆ ⅓ cup raw honey or pure maple syrup
- ◆ 2 tablespoons almond butter
- ◆ 1 tablespoon vanilla extract
- ◆ 3 tablespoons coconut oil
- ◆ ⅓ cup coconut flour
- ◆ 2 cups almond flour
- ◆ 1½ teaspoons ground cinnamon
- ◆ 1 teaspoon ground nutmeg
- ◆ 1 teaspoon baking soda
- ◆ 1 teaspoon sea salt
- ◆ 1 cup walnut pieces, chopped (toast if desired)

Directions:

1. Turn on your slow cooker to HIGH while you get your ingredients ready.
2. Spray or apply coconut oil to the sides and bottom of your loaf pan.
3. In a blender, put in the bananas, eggs, honey, almond butter, vanilla, and coconut oil.
4. Allow the blender to run on low or medium while you mix up the dry ingredients in a bowl.
5. Add the banana mixture to the combined dry ingredients and mix until thoroughly blended.
6. Pour the batter into the loaf pan.
7. Place the lid on your slow cooker, using a couple of toothpicks to prop it up to reduce any condensation.
8. Cook on HIGH for 2 hours.

9. Using a toothpick, check for doneness.
10. Remove from the slow cooker and place the pan on a cooling rack for 15 minutes.
11. Using a knife, scrape the sides loose and gently invert the bread pan so the loaf is on the cooling rack.
12. Allow to cool completely.
13. Slice and butter if desired.

APPLE CINNAMON BREAD

Ingredients:

- 3 eggs (bring to room temperature)
- ¼ cup coconut oil, melted
- 2 tablespoons raw honey or pure maple syrup
- ¼ cup unsweetened applesauce
- 3 tablespoons coconut flour
- 1 cup almond flour
- 1 heaping tablespoon cinnamon
- ½ teaspoon baking soda
- ½ teaspoon sea salt
- 1 large, tart apple, peeled, cored, and diced

Directions:

1. Turn on your slow cooker to HIGH while you get your ingredients ready.
2. Spray or apply coconut oil to the sides and bottom of your loaf pan.
3. In a blender, put the eggs, coconut oil, honey, and applesauce.
4. Allow the blender to run on low or medium while you mix up the dry ingredients in a bowl.
5. Combine dry ingredients and coat apples pieces with them.
6. Pour the ingredients in the blender into the dry ingredients and mix thoroughly.
7. Pour the batter into the loaf pan.
8. Place the lid on your slow cooker, using a couple of toothpicks to prop it up to reduce any condensation.
9. Cook on HIGH for 2 hours.
10. Using a toothpick, check for doneness.
11. Remove from the slow cooker and place the pan on a cooling rack for 15 minutes.

12. Using a knife, scrape the sides loose and gently invert the bread pan so the loaf is on the cooling rack.
13. Allow to cool completely.
14. Slice and butter if desired.

ZUCCHINI AND CARROT BREAD

Ingredients:

- 2 large eggs (room temperature)
- ¼ cup raw honey or pure maple syrup
- ¼ cup coconut oil
- 1 teaspoon vanilla extract
- 1 tablespoon coconut flour
- 2 cups almond flour
- 1 tablespoon ground cinnamon
- ½ teaspoon baking soda
- ½ teaspoon sea salt
- 1 carrot, grated (½ cup)
- 1 zucchini, grated (¾ cup)
- ¼ cup raisins

Directions:

1. Turn on your slow cooker to HIGH while you get your ingredients ready.
2. Spray or apply coconut oil to the sides and bottom of your loaf pan.
3. In a blender, put the eggs, honey, oil, and vanilla.
4. Allow the blender to run on low or medium while you mix up the dry ingredients in a bowl.
5. Add the wet ingredients into the dry ingredients and mix thoroughly.
6. Stir in the carrot, zucchini, and raisins.
7. Pour the batter into the loaf pan.
8. Place the lid on your slow cooker, using a couple of toothpicks to prop it up to reduce any condensation.
9. Cook on HIGH for 2 hours.
10. Using a toothpick, check for doneness.
11. Remove from the slow cooker and place the pan on a cooling rack for 15 minutes.
12. Using a knife, scrape the sides loose and gently invert the bread pan so the loaf is on the cooling rack.
13. Allow to cool completely.
14. Slice and butter if desired.

ALMOND BREAD WITH COCONUT

Ingredients:

- ♦ 6 large eggs (room temperature)
- ♦ 1 large ripe banana
- ♦ ⅜ cup coconut milk
- ♦ 1 teaspoon vanilla extract
- ♦ 2 tablespoons coconut oil
- ♦ 1 cup coconut flour
- ♦ ¼ cup flax seed meal
- ♦ ½ cup almond flour
- ♦ 1 teaspoon sea salt
- ♦ 1½ teaspoons baking soda
- ♦ 1 cup shredded coconut

Directions:

1. Turn on your slow cooker to HIGH while you get your ingredients ready.
2. Spray or apply coconut oil to the sides and bottom of your loaf pan.
3. In a blender, put the eggs, banana, coconut milk, vanilla, and coconut oil.
4. Allow the blender to run on low or medium while you mix up the dry ingredients in a bowl.
5. Add the wet ingredients into the dry ingredients and mix thoroughly.
6. Stir in the shredded coconut.
7. Pour the batter into the loaf pan.
8. Place the lid on your slow cooker, using a couple of toothpicks to prop it up to reduce any condensation.
9. Cook on HIGH for 2 hours.
10. Using a toothpick, check for doneness.
11. Remove from the slow cooker and place the pan on a cooling rack for 15 minutes.
12. Using a knife, scrape the sides loose and gently invert the bread pan so the loaf is on the cooling rack.
13. Allow to cool completely.
14. Slice and butter if desired.

About the Author

Amelia Simons is a food enthusiast, wife, and mother of five. Frustrated with traditional dieting advice, she stumbled upon the Paleolithic lifestyle of eating and has never looked back. Without bothering to count calories or stress about endless hours of exercise, eating the Paleolithic way enabled Amelia and her husband to effortlessly drop pounds and lower their cholesterol.

Amelia now enjoys sharing the Paleolithic philosophy with friends and readers and finding new ways to turn favorite recipes into healthy alternatives.

Additional Resources

Be sure to check out my other titles:

Gluten-Free Slow Cooker: Easy Recipes for a Gluten Free Diet

Paleolithic Slow Cooker: Simple & Healthy Gluten-Free Recipes

Going Paleolithic: A Quick Start Guide for a Gluten-Free Diet

4 Weeks of Fabulous Paleolithic Breakfasts

4 MORE Weeks of Fabulous Paleolithic Breakfasts

4 Weeks of Fabulous Paleolithic Lunches

4 Weeks of Fabulous Paleolithic Dinners

The Ultimate Paleolithic Collection

METRIC AND IMPERIAL CONVERSIONS

(These conversions are rounded for convenience)

Ingredient	Cups/Tablespoons/Teaspoons	Ounces	Grams/Milliliters
Butter	1 cup=16 tablespoons= 2 sticks	8 ounces	230 grams
Cream cheese	1 tablespoon	0.5 ounce	14.5 grams
Cheese, shredded	1 cup	4 ounces	110 grams
Cornstarch	1 tablespoon	0.3 ounce	8 grams
Flour, all-purpose	1 cup/1 tablespoon	4.5 ounces/0.3 ounce	125 grams/8 grams
Flour, whole wheat	1 cup	4 ounces	120 grams
Fruit, dried	1 cup	4 ounces	120 grams
Fruits or veggies, chopped	1 cup	5 to 7 ounces	145 to 200 grams
Fruits or veggies, puréed	1 cup	8.5 ounces	245 grams
Honey, maple syrup, or corn syrup	1 tablespoon	.75 ounce	20 grams
Liquids: cream, milk, water, or juice	1 cup	8 fluid ounces	240 milliliters
Oats	1 cup	5.5 ounces	150 grams
Salt	1 teaspoon	0.2 ounces	6 grams
Spices: cinnamon, cloves, ginger, or nutmeg (ground)	1 teaspoon	0.2 ounce	5 milliliters
Sugar, brown, firmly packed	1 cup	7 ounces	200 grams
Sugar, white	1 cup/1 tablespoon	7 ounces/0.5 ounce	200 grams/12.5 grams
Vanilla extract	1 teaspoon	0.2 ounce	4 grams

OVEN TEMPERATURES

Fahrenheit	Celcius	Gas Mark
225°	110°	¼
250°	120°	½
275°	140°	1
300°	150°	2
325°	160°	3
350°	180°	4
375°	190°	5
400°	200°	6
425°	220°	7
450°	230°	8

ALSO AVAILABLE

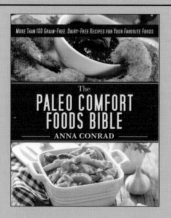

The Paleo Comfort Foods Bible

More Than 100 Grain-Free, Dairy-Free Recipes for Your Favorite Foods

by Anna Conrad

If you think the increasingly popular caveman diet is good for your health but a bit depressing for your taste buds, this is the book that will change your perspective on the paleo diet forever. Now you can enjoy all your favorite comfort foods without sacrificing the terrific health benefits of a grain-free, dairy-free diet.

When chef and caterer Anna Conrad was asked to provide paleo recipes for a fitness group's twenty-eight-day paleo challenge, she was a little skeptical. Could an athlete—or even an average person—really maintain a balanced body without any grains or dairy? Before agreeing to the job, she decided to follow the diet for two weeks to see how she felt. In that short amount of time, she lost eight pounds without feeling hungry or deprived, and her blood pressure, heart rate, and cholesterol all stayed within healthy limits. She gladly provided the recipes and now offers a paleo menu as a regular part of her catering business. In this book, she offers delicious comfort food recipes, including:

- Chicken pot pie
- Creamed spinach
- Meatloaf
- Rueben sandwich
- Shrimp bisque
- Spaghetti carbonara
- And more!

$17.95 Hardcover • ISBN 978-1-62873-620-5

ALSO AVAILABLE

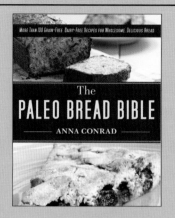

The Paleo Bread Bible

More Than 100 Grain-Free, Dairy-Free Recipes for Wholesome, Delicious Bread

by Anna Conrad

When chef and caterer Anna Conrad was asked to provide paleo recipes for a fitness group's twenty-eight-day paleo challenge, she was a little skeptical. Could an athlete—or even an average person—really maintain a balanced body without any grains or dairy? Before agreeing to the job, she decided to follow the diet for two weeks to see how she felt. In that short amount of time, she lost eight pounds without feeling hungry or deprived, and her blood pressure, heart rate, and cholesterol all stayed within healthy limits. She gladly provided the recipes and now offers a paleo menu as a regular part of her catering business.

But what about bread? How can you make bread without grains? In this book, Conrad teaches how to make wholesome and satisfying breads with almond flour, coconut flour, and a host of other delicious, nongrain flours. Recipes include:

- Almond sandwich bread

- Coconut sandwich bread

- Rosemary and olive oil bread

- Sweet potato rosemary focaccia

- Savory bacon and scallion muffins

- Molasses brown bread

- And many more!

$17.95 Hardcover • ISBN 978-1-62873-619-9

ALSO AVAILABLE

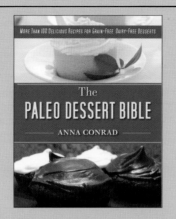

The Paleo Dessert Bible

More Than 100 Delicious Recipes for Grain-Free, Dairy-Free Desserts

by Anna Conrad

By now we all know that the paleo diet yields amazing results for weight loss and overall well-being. But even the most health-conscious among us want to treat ourselves once in a while to something sweet and indulgent. What if we could indulge without cheating on the diet? In this book, readers will find more than one hundred recipes for amazing desserts that will leave you feeling satisfied, energized, and healthy.

When chef and caterer Anna Conrad was asked to provide paleo recipes for a fitness group's twenty-eight-day paleo challenge, she was a little skeptical. Could an athlete—or even an average person—really maintain a balanced body without any grains or dairy? Before agreeing to the job, she decided to follow the diet for two weeks to see how she felt. In that short amount of time, she lost eight pounds without feeling hungry or deprived, and her blood pressure, heart rate, and cholesterol all stayed within healthy limits. She gladly provided the recipes and now offers a paleo menu as a regular part of her catering business. In this book, she offers delicious dessert recipes, including:

- Almond butter cookies
- Bread pudding
- Chewy chocolate cookies
- Chocolate fudge cake
- Lemon squares
- Pecan bars
- And more!

$17.95 Hardcover • ISBN 978-1-62873-621-2

ALSO AVAILABLE

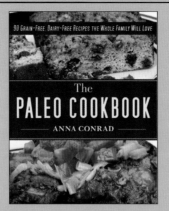

The Paleo Cookbook

90 Grain-Free, Dairy-Free Recipes the Whole Family Will Love

by Anna Conrad

When chef and caterer Anna Conrad was asked to provide paleo recipes for a fitness group's twenty-eight-day paleo challenge, she was a little skeptical. Could an athlete—or even an average person—really maintain a balanced body without any grains or dairy? Before agreeing to the job, she decided to follow the diet for two weeks to see how she felt. In that short amount of time, she lost eight pounds without feeling hungry or deprived, and her blood pressure, heart rate, and cholesterol all stayed within healthy limits. She gladly provided the recipes and now offers a paleo menu as a regular part of her catering business.

In this book, Conrad explains the basics of the paleo diet and then provides ninety delicious recipes for every meal of the day, plus some snacks and desserts. She also includes the menu for her twenty-eight-day paleo challenge for those just starting the paleo lifestyle. Recipes include:

- Pumpkin spice muffins
- Basil pesto stir-fry
- Garlic lime chicken
- Pork tenderloin with apples and onions
- Bison chili
- Baked fish with asparagus and roasted beets
- Stuffed portobellos
- Blueberry citrus pound cake
- And many more!

$17.95 Hardcover • ISBN 978-1-62636-394-6

ALSO AVAILABLE

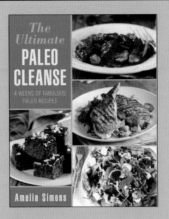

The Ultimate Paleo Cleanse

4 Weeks of Fabulous Paleo Recipes

by Amelia Simons

The first step to becoming healthier can often be the hardest to take. *The Ultimate Paleo Cleanse* helps ease this transition by providing a fantastic starting point with a detailed menu covering breakfast, lunch, and dinner ideas over a four-week period. There's no better way to begin your road to success than with these simple, flavorful meals.

Within *The Ultimate Paleo Cleanse*, readers will find a wide range of recipes covering every meal from breakfast to lunch and dinner, including scrumptious grain-free, gluten-free appetizers and desserts. Some of the delicious choices you'll find in this collection are:

- Delicious quiche cups

- Hearty sautéed peach salad

- Grilled chicken breasts with garlic

- Garlic hummus

- Chocolate coconut pudding

- And many different muffin, bread, and pancake recipes!

Also included in this cookbook is an overview of the paleo lifestyle that will give you a quick, easy-to-follow guide of the recommended foods and the ones to avoid. Improving your health has never been easier!

$17.95 Hardcover • ISBN 978-1-62914-552-5

ALSO AVAILABLE

The Paleo Effect
More Than 150 All-Natural Recipes for a Grain-Free, Dairy-Free Lifestyle
by Meghan Little and Angel Ayala Torres

With the overwhelming number of frozen dinners and processed foods that line our grocery store aisles, it's easy to see how we've forgotten what "real food" tastes like. Our bodies are left undernourished as our weight rapidly increases, while words like "diabetes" and "obesity" flood the media. The time has come to embrace a new lifestyle, not another diet: a lifestyle where the foods we consume are not based on calories or points, but instead on pure ingredients that our bodies need.

It's time for a healthier you with *The Paleo Effect*. Authors and bloggers Meghan Little and Angel Ayala Torres share with us simple, wholesome recipes free of dairy, grains, and processed sugars and fats. Join the paleo revolution and relearn how to nourish your body! Say good-bye to the processed life that has left so many overweight, malnourished, and sick; and say hello to increased energy, weight loss, a healthier immune system, and so much more!

Check out some of these paleo lifestyle flavor-packed recipes:

- Wild-caught salmon with mashed sweet potatoes
- Puerto Rican arañitas, a fried green plantain appetizer
- Grain-free, dairy-free blueberry muffins
- Chicken pot pie, a grain-free comfort food

Make *The Paleo Effect* your go-to guide with over 150 recipes and full-color photographs, as well as a full array of how-to guides, quick tips, and seasonal eating recommendations. It's time to relearn how to cook the way Mother Nature intended with *The Paleo Effect*.

$19.95 Hardcover • ISBN 978-1-62636-162-1

ALSO AVAILABLE

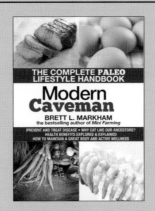

Modern Caveman

The Complete Paleo Lifestyle Handbook

by Brett L. Markham

Nature spent millions of years forging genetic code so that you could be strong, fit, and healthy throughout your life. Yet, when we look around, we see an epidemic of obesity, autoimmune diseases, young people with diabetes, and people succumbing to heart disease in early middle age. Why?

Though "nature versus nurture" has long been at the heart of debates concerning psychology and sociology, it is only in the past few years that the idea of conforming our diet and exercise to our genome has gained traction. And it is precisely this idea that holds the key to unlocking your potential to be happier, healthier, and more fit than most can imagine is possible.

Why didn't our Paleolithic forebears suffer from tooth decay, yet dentists' offices are ubiquitous in our society? Why is it that middle-aged men who are gobbling whole grains by the bushel and eating tofu to banish meat from their diets are still requiring expensive statin drug prescriptions to control their cholesterol? *Modern Caveman* tries to answer these questions, describing an evolutionarily healthful lifestyle of diet, living patterns, and exercise that is easily adopted and maintained throughout life. Are you ready to fulfill the true destiny that nature has given you? *Modern Caveman* holds the answer to achieving and maintaining a great body, strength, energy, and active wellness right into a healthy old age with dramatically decreased risks of "diseases of civilization."

$16.95 Paperback • ISBN 978-1-62873-715-8